Get a grip!

Get a grip!

How Old Testament saints dealt with tough times

Anthony T. Selvaggio

PUBLISHING WITH A MISSION

EP BOOKS
Faverdale North, Darlington, DL3 0PH, England

www.epbooks.org

e-mail: sales@epbooks.org

EP BOOKS USA
P. O. Box 614, Carlisle, PA 17013, USA

www.epbooks.us

e-mail: usasales@epbooks.org

First published 2010

British Library Cataloguing in Publication Data available

ISBN-13 978-0-85234-724-9   ISBN 0-85234-724-3

Printed and bound in the United States of America by Versa Press Inc., East Peoria, IL.

*This book is dedicated to the memory
of my father-in-law Rev. Ivan G. Kellogg.
Although many difficult things happened to him,
he never ceased serving, praising and loving his Lord.*

Contents

Introduction

Now these things happened to them

*These things happened to them as examples and
were written down as warnings for us,
on whom the fulfilment of the ages has come*
(1 Corinthians 10:11).

I was going through an extremely difficult period in the
ministry. It was perhaps the lowest point I had ever reached.
I was distraught over the circumstances and I began to
question my calling and usefulness to God. Then my phone rang.
It was a friend calling. He was a pastor in a sister denomination
who had experienced his own set of wounds in the ministry. I
began to share my burdens with him and he ministered to me.
He used his own experiences to help me, but he also drew from
the Scriptures. He particularly used the example of Joseph. He
reminded me that Joseph really wasn't useful to God until after
he had been hurt and forsaken.

That phone call was tremendously helpful to me. It enabled
me to change my attitude and to deal more effectively with
the challenges I was facing. Throughout this difficult period

I continued to remind myself of the example of Joseph. I encouraged myself with the thought that, like Joseph, God was using my trials to make me more useful to him and to others. The Old Testament example of Joseph comforted and guided me through a very difficult time in my life.

After this experience, I began to think a great deal about the lives of the Old Testament saints. I realized that one of the unique aspects of the Old Testament is how honestly it portrays the lives of these believers. We see them, 'warts and all'. We watch them go through marital and family problems. We witness their triumphs and their sins. I also realized that many of their struggles are very similar to our own. Even though they lived thousands of years ago, our lives are really not so different from theirs. I began to consider how their lives could be used to assist believers today as we journey our way through the maze of this life.

This book is the fruit of that exploration. In this book I share what a select group of Old Testament saints can teach us about a variety of common problems ranging from failure to fear. This book is an effort to extract lessons from their lives so that we can better live our own lives.

The problem of the Old Testament saints

Yet writing this book was no easy task because it forced me to wrestle with one of the thorniest issues in biblical interpretation and preaching — how to deal properly with the lives of the Old Testament saints. This issue has sparked a great debate in the church. Two opposing viewpoints have emerged as a result.

The first is called the 'exemplary' approach and it emphasizes the importance of understanding the Old Testament saints as examples for us. At its worst, the exemplary approach can easily degrade into pure 'moralism' in which the *sole* function of these saints is to teach us basic moral lessons. This viewpoint gives rise to sermons with titles such as, 'Dare to be a Daniel' or 'Slay your Goliath'. In its most extreme form, the exemplary approach entirely neglects the role of the Old Testament saint in directing us to the person and work of Jesus Christ. In the exemplary approach Jesus is often missing.

The second approach is known as the 'redemptive-historical' approach. This approach emphasizes identifying the role of the Old Testament saints in the unfolding of redemptive history and specifically focusing on how they point us to Jesus Christ. At first glance this seems like a very attractive approach, but it also has a downside. Sometimes the redemptive-historical approach can lead to predictably similar sounding sermons which survey the grand landscape of the Bible, but never really minister to the needs and problems of God's people. In the redemptive-historical approach the real life of the believer is sometimes missing.

In the process of researching and writing this book, I came to the conclusion that neither of these approaches is satisfactory. I became convinced that a synthesis of the two views is necessary. The redemptive-historical approach is right to continually point us to Christ as the centre of the entire Bible, but the exemplary approach is right to remind us that the Bible is given to us to help us live faithfully in response to the work of Christ. The Old Testament saints were real people, not mere types. Yes, their ultimate significance is found in how they reveal Jesus Christ, but that does not mean they cannot also teach us important lessons about living the Christian life.

The New Testament solution to the problem

Fortunately, the New Testament solves the problem of the Old Testament saints for us. As is often the case, the Bible provides us with the best guide to solving matters of interpretation. When one surveys how the human authors of the New Testament dealt with the Old Testament saints it becomes abundantly clear that both of these approaches have merit. The New Testament makes it clear that the saints of the Old Testament serve both as types of Jesus Christ and as examples for us.

The New Testament frequently uses Old Testament saints as types which point us to Jesus. For example, the ministries of Moses and Elijah serve as types of the ministry of Jesus. The kingship of David is used as a type of the kingship of Jesus Christ. The New Testament teaches us that Jonah's three days in the belly of the fish point us to Jesus' resurrection; and that King Solomon's wisdom points us to the even wiser King Jesus.

But with equal clarity and conviction, the New Testament also treats the Old Testament saints as examples for us. For instance, the writer to the Hebrews uses a litany of Old Testament saints in Hebrews 11 as examples to us of how to persevere through the trials of this age. The writer to the Hebrews also uses the generation that died in the wilderness as an example to us of the type of unfaithfulness we should avoid. Similarly, James uses Old Testament saints like Abraham, Rahab, Elijah and Job as examples in his epistle. The apostle Paul also used Old Testament saints as examples for us. We see this particularly in his first epistle to the Corinthians.

> The New Testament makes it clear that the saints of the Old Testament serve both as types of Jesus Christ and as examples for us.

In 1 Corinthians 10, the apostle Paul warns the congregation at Corinth, and us, against the dangers of engaging in idolatry. To illustrate his point he used the example of the generation in the wilderness. That generation had engaged in idolatry and as a result they died in the wilderness. Paul admonished the church at Corinth by using them as an example: 'We should not test the Lord, *as some of them did* — and were killed by snakes. And do not grumble, *as some of them did* — and were killed by the destroying angel' (1 Corinthians 10:9-10, emphasis mine). Paul made their exemplary use explicit by stating: 'These things happened to them as examples and were written down as warnings for us, on whom the fulfilment of the ages has come' (1 Corinthians 10:11).

Paul declared that the things that happened to the Old Testament saints were not only given to us to reveal Jesus Christ, but also to serve as 'examples' and 'warnings' for us. The things that happened to them were specifically tailored by God to be useful and instructive to New Covenant believers as they live the Christian life. We are those upon 'whom the fulfilment of the ages has come' (10:11).

The New Testament teaches us that the Old Testament saints serve both as types and examples. So what we need is a balanced view that treats the Old Testament saints as real people who can teach us real lessons, but also never loses sight of the fact that their ultimate significance is found in pointing us to Jesus. One theologian summarized this type of balanced approach as follows:

> Our fathers knew very well that redemptive history is a unified structure with Christ at its center, but they still felt free to treat separately (using biblical givens) certain persons described in Scripture, to picture them psychologically, to speak of their struggles and trials, their strengths and weaknesses, and then to draw parallels between the experiences of the Bible saints and the struggles of believers today. Without any hesitation our fathers held up the virtues of the biblical persons as an example to all, but also their sins and weaknesses as a warning.[1]

This is the approach that I have attempted to employ in this book.

Now these things happened to them

It is my desire that through this book you will see how the things that happened to the saints of the Old Testament can help you deal with a series of problems which are common to us all. I want you to see that they were real people and that you have much in common with them. But I also want you to see that they all serve as signposts directing us to our glorious Lord and Saviour Jesus Christ.

So let us begin our journey and endeavour to benefit from the things written down about these saints. Let us go forward being mindful of Paul's words: 'These things happened to them as examples and were written down as warnings for us, on whom the fulfilment of the ages has come' (1 Corinthians 10:11). Let us gaze into the lives of these saints and see what they can teach us about living the Christian life, but let us also allow these saints to escort us into the presence of Jesus Christ.

1.

What happened to Abraham:

dealing with waiting

The Lord had said to Abram, 'Leave your country, your people and
your father's household and go to the land I will show you. I will
make you into a great nation and I will bless you; I will make your
name great, and you will be a blessing. I will bless those who bless
you, and whoever curses you I will curse; and all peoples on earth
will be blessed through you'
(Genesis 12:1-3).

One of my besetting sins is impatience. I struggle with
waiting. I want my 'to do' list to be done yesterday.
I want my problems solved immediately. I want to
achieve my goals and dreams now. I hate waiting. I'm nearly
forty years old now and I've only slightly improved in this area
from when I was two years old! In fact, my son James is two
years old and I find an embarrassing resemblance between his
lack of patience and my own! I simply struggle with waiting.

How about you? Have you ever struggled with waiting for
something? Perhaps you are waiting for something right now.

Maybe you are waiting for the blessing of children, or the blessing of finding a spouse. Maybe you are waiting to hear about a job, or whether you were accepted into a college or university. Maybe you are waiting for the results of an important test. Perhaps you are waiting to realize a life-long dream. Do you struggle with waiting? Are you impatient?

Sometimes we dismiss impatience as a minor character flaw, but the Bible tells us that it is much more than that. The Bible teaches us that impatience is evidence of discontentment with the providence of God. Impatience with God is sinful and it breeds other sins. Consider what one Puritan theologian wrote about the consequences of the sin of impatience:

> While being impatient, many sins merge together. An impatient person is a breeding ground for all manner of corruptions which grievously pollute the soul. There is unbelief toward God's promises, lovelessness and stubbornness toward God's will, pride (as if they were superior), envy and vengefulness toward their neighbour, and a holding in esteem the things of this world.[1]

God expects us to trust in him and his timing. He expects us to be patient. He expects us to wait on him. Therefore, it is important for us to learn how to cultivate patience in our lives. It is important for us to learn how to deal with waiting in a godly manner.

One place to look for some guidance on how to deal with waiting is the life of the patriarch Abraham. Abraham had to deal with *a lot* of waiting in his life. One day God unilaterally intervened in Abraham's life and made two amazing promises to him. God promised him land and offspring (Genesis 12:1-3). He told Abraham that he would receive great things, but what God didn't tell him was exactly *when* he would receive them. God provided no timetable to Abraham. Instead, he called upon Abraham to wait. In this chapter we will survey the life of Abraham to see what it teaches us about dealing with waiting.

Waiting for the land

When God called Abraham he promised to give him land: 'The LORD had said to Abram, "Leave your country, your people and your father's household and *go to the land I will show you*"' (Genesis 12:1, emphasis mine). Essentially, God told Abraham to pack his bags, leave his home and move to an unknown country. Can you imagine doing such a thing? Leaving all you know and moving to who knows where? But Abraham did it. He didn't hesitate. He didn't ask questions. Instead, he quickly gathered his possessions, assembled his family and set out for the land that God had promised to give him (Genesis 12:5).

Canaanites were in the land

When Abraham finally arrived at his new home he was immediately confronted with an unpleasant surprise — someone was already living there! Genesis 12:6 makes this simple declaration: 'Canaanites were in the land.' Now, just pause and consider what Abraham must have been thinking at this moment. In a great act of faith he left his home and his career to follow God to this new land and when he gets there he finds that the land is already occupied! It's analogous to someone promising to give you a beautiful beach house on a desert island, so you leave your job, sell your house, pack up your belongings, gather your family, travel many hundreds of miles, and, when you finally arrive at the house, you discover that another family is already residing there. How would you feel at that moment? If you are anything like me, I think you would feel discouraged, disappointed and despondent. My guess is that Abraham probably had similar feelings.

Get a grip!

Famine was in the land

When Abraham spotted the Canaanites living in the land promised to him it must have dawned on him that possessing this land might take a bit longer than he initially anticipated. So Abraham began his waiting. He pitched his tent, built an altar to worship God and God began to prosper him.

But just when it seemed that things were improving for Abraham in his new home, we read of the following bad news in Genesis 12:10:

> Now there was a famine in the land, and Abram went down to Egypt to live there for a while because the famine was severe.

This great land of promise, for which Abraham had given up all, was now not only occupied by Canaanites, but it was also filled with famine! The famine was so severe that Abraham had to leave the land and travel to Egypt. He was forced to take one giant leap away from his inheritance. As he moved his family to Egypt, it must have been abundantly clear that he would have to wait a little longer to possess this land.

War was in the land

Eventually, Abraham returned to the land, pitched his tent and built a new altar to the Lord. But just after he returned home he faced a new threat to his possession of the land — war (Genesis 14).

Abraham then entered into battle against foreign kings who had taken his nephew Lot prisoner. He proved victorious in battle and he liberated Lot. Abraham acquired even greater wealth through the spoils of war, but he still did not possess the land. Then, upon the heels of his great victory, God provided

Abraham with some more information regarding the timing of his inheritance:

> On that day the LORD made a covenant with Abram and said, '*To your descendants* I give this land, from the river of Egypt to the great river, the Euphrates'
> (Genesis 15:18, emphasis mine).

God informed Abraham that he would not possess the land during his lifetime. Instead he would come to possess it through his descendants. Once again, Abraham was told to wait for the promises of God.

A stranger in the promised land

Abraham left everything to follow God. He was seeking a better country. But when he got there he encountered Canaanites, famine and war. He encountered obstacles and delays. He waited his entire life and never realized the fulfilment of the promise. Sixty long years after being called out of Ur of the Chaldees, Abraham described himself as a 'stranger' and an 'alien' in the land that God had promised to give him (Genesis 23:3-4). After his wife Sarah's death, Abraham even had to purchase a burial plot for her from the Hittites. In other words, he had to pay for a small part of the land that was his by divine promise!

When Abraham died, he was buried in the same plot he had purchased for Sarah. He died possessing only his own grave. He lived every day of his life waiting for the fulfilment of a promise that was never ultimately realized in his lifetime. He died waiting for the land.

But Abraham's struggle with waiting was not limited to the promise of the land. God had given Abraham a second promise. He had promised Abraham offspring. But Abraham would have to wait for the fulfilment of this promise as well.

Waiting for the seed

When God first called Abraham, his name was actually 'Abram', which means 'exalted father'. God eventually changed his name to 'Abraham', which means 'father of a multitude'. Both of these names indicate that fatherhood was central to Abraham's destiny. But when Abraham first arrived in the promised land he was childless. He was the father of no one and he wasn't getting any younger. In fact, Abraham was so concerned about his lack of offspring that he contemplated making one of his servants his legal heir.

It was at this point that God intervened and promised Abraham that he would indeed be a father:

> Then the word of the LORD came to him: 'This man will not be your heir, but a son coming from your own body will be your heir.' He took him outside and said, 'Look up at the heavens and count the stars — if indeed you can count them.' Then he said to him, 'So shall your offspring be'
> (Genesis 15:4-5).

God not only promised Abraham that he would have *a* son, but that he would have *many* sons and daughters, as many as the stars in the heavens. Abraham received a tremendous promise, but once again he would be forced to wait to see it fulfilled.

The mistake of Ishmael

The glorious promise Abraham received in Genesis 15 is followed abruptly by this declaration in the first verse of Genesis 16: 'Now Sarai, Abram's wife, had borne him no children.' God had promised, but nothing was happening. Sarah was not getting pregnant and the waiting was beginning to take its toll on Abraham, and even more so on Sarah.

Sarah was now eighty-six years old and, despite God's promise, she was still barren. Her growing impatience led her to rationalize a new plan to see God's promise fulfilled in their lives. She decided that maybe God intended Abraham's promised son to be conceived by a different mother. Becoming convinced of this, Sarah goaded her husband into having relations with her handmaid Hagar. Abraham did not resist his wife's persuasion and consented to participate in her scheme.

Initially, their plan seemed to be incredibly successful. Hagar became pregnant and bore Abraham a son, which they called Ishmael. Ultimately, however, the plan would turn out to be anything but a success. Jealousy began to foment between Sarah and Hagar. Eventually, this jealousy gave rise to hatred, and Sarah demanded that Hagar and Ishmael be banished. One day, however, Ishmael would bear descendants that would trouble Abraham's true descendants for generations. Abraham's struggle to wait for the promise would cost him, and his descendants, dearly.

God eventually made it clear to Abraham that Ishmael was not the son of promise. In Genesis 17, God informed Abraham and Sarah that the true son of promise would be born to both of them and that he would be named 'Isaac' (v. 19). Abraham was a hundred years old at this time and Sarah was ninety years old. God's declaration regarding Isaac made it clear that Abraham's waiting was still not over.

The test of Isaac

Finally, in Genesis 21, we learn that Abraham realized the promise of offspring as Isaac is born to Sarah. But for Abraham the waiting was still not over. Remember, the promise to Abraham went far beyond just one son. Abraham was promised many sons. He was promised that he would be the father of a multitude. After the birth of Isaac, however, Abraham spent fifteen years with just one son. He must have been wondering, 'Where are the multitudes?'

But as Abraham was waiting for more sons, God intervened in his life and commanded him to sacrifice his one and only son! Can you imagine what this must have been like for Abraham? Waiting all those years to finally realize one true heir and then God demands that he return this heir to him! Abraham found himself waiting again, but this time he was waiting to sacrifice his own son.

Ultimately, God stayed the knife-bearing hand of Abraham and spared the life of Isaac. God graciously accepted a substitute sacrifice which he providentially provided in the form of a ram caught in the thicket. Isaac was preserved and so was the promise made to Abraham.

Abraham did have more offspring after the birth of Isaac. He had six additional sons with his second wife Keturah. But Abraham died with a modest number of descendants, certainly not as numerous as the stars in the sky. Abraham died waiting for the fulness of the promise God made to him. He died waiting for a multitude of offspring.

Learning from the life of Abraham

As we've seen in this chapter, Abraham was given two marvellous promises: the promise of land and the promise of offspring. He did not receive immediate gratification on either of these promises. He died with a burial plot and eight sons. Even these partial fulfilments were only received after waiting many years. Abraham's hopes and longings languished for years amid the trials of his life. Like Abraham, we too often find ourselves struggling with waiting for the things for which we long. Our hopes and dreams often seem afar off in the timeline of our lives. Like Abraham, we become discouraged and impatient.

Abraham's life is given to us for our instruction and it has some lessons for us regarding waiting. Abraham's life teaches us in both positive and negative ways. Let's start with what Abraham got right.

What Abraham got right: faithfulness

The most important thing that Abraham God right in his life was that when God promised him something Abraham responded by believing God. Abraham showed tremendous faith throughout his life. He believed God despite the lack of present possession of the things promised to him. He believed in the face of many obstacles. Genesis 15:6 provides us with great testimony to Abraham's faith: 'Abram believed the LORD, and he credited it to him as righteousness.' What Abraham got right was that he exercised faith as he waited for fulfilment.

When we begin to talk about Abraham's faith we must make sure that we understand its ultimate source. Abraham's faith was not self-generated or self-cultivated. God gave it to him and God nurtured it continually. Just consider how many times God intervened in Abraham's life at crucial moments to reiterate the promises to him. God declares and repeats promises to Abraham in Genesis 12, 15, 17 and 22. He gave Abraham the visible sign of circumcision to complement his spoken promises to provide further assurance to him. God entered into covenant with Abraham (Genesis 15) and even swore an oath to him (Hebrews 6:13-15). God does similar things for us while we wait. God covenants with us. He speaks to us through the Word preached and he gives us visible signs of his promises in baptism and the Lord's Supper. The lesson of Abraham's life

> The lesson of Abraham's life is not ultimately that he was so faithful to God, but rather that God was so faithful to him.

is not ultimately that he was so faithful to God, but rather that God was so faithful to him.

Keeping in mind that God was the ultimate source of Abraham's faith, Scripture nonetheless commends Abraham for living faithfully. Abraham did not squander God's gift of faith. Consider the following testimonies to Abraham's faithfulness found in the New Testament:

Abraham's faith in leaving his home: '*By faith* Abraham, when called to go to a place he would later receive as his inheritance, obeyed and went, even though he did not know where he was going,' (Hebrews 11:8, emphasis mine).

Abraham's faith regarding offspring: 'Yet *he did not waver through unbelief* regarding the promise of God, but was *strengthened in his faith* and gave glory to God, being fully persuaded that God had power to do what he had promised' (Romans 4:20-21, emphasis mine).

Abraham's faith regarding sacrificing Isaac: '*By faith* Abraham, when God tested him, offered Isaac as a sacrifice' (Hebrews 11:17).

It is no wonder that Abraham is referred to as the 'father of the faithful'. At very crucial moments throughout his life, Abraham lived by faith and not by sight.

Abraham's life of faith reminds us that when we are waiting for something we must believe God and trust in him. We must exercise faith even when things seem bleak and impossible. Remember, believing in things that we cannot presently see is the exact definition of biblical faith, 'Now faith is being sure of what we hope for and *certain of what we do not see*' (Hebrews 11:1, emphasis mine). This is what Abraham did while he was waiting and it is what we must do as well. Abraham's life teaches us to be faithful while we wait.

What Abraham got wrong: forcing fulfilment

While the totality of Abraham's life was marked by faithfulness, he was not perfect in exercising faith. At times, he failed to trust in God and this led him to make bad decisions. The clearest example of this is his role in creating Ishmael. Abraham longed for a male heir. This longing was confirmed through divine promise. But Abraham allowed this divine promise to morph into a personal sense of entitlement. This in turn allowed him to convince himself that he should force the fulfilment of this promise in his own way. The result was Ishmael.

It is very easy for us to repeat Abraham's mistake by rationalizing ways to force the fulfilment of our own desires and dreams. We grow weary of waiting for God and our impatience leads us to hatch our own plans. It is often the case that the plans we concoct are very plausible and reasonable. They often involve no overtly sinful acts. They can be justified on all the facts. This is exactly what happened in Abraham's case when he agreed to the plan of using Hagar as the means to realize the promise of descendants. Iain Duguid comments on the seeming plausibility and reasonableness of Abraham's actions:

> In taking Hagar as his wife, Abram was motivated not by lust, but by an eager desire to see God's purpose fulfilled. After all, though the promise had identified him as the father, Sarai had not yet been explicitly designated as the mother of Abram's descendants. Furthermore, the taking of a concubine was a socially accepted custom in that day. All parties involved were consenting adults, so why not? The idea seemed so reasonable, as Satan's shortcuts always do![2]

Abraham forged a quite reasonable plan to attain his desires, but it was not God's plan. This is the core of Abraham's mistake — allowing impatience to breed disobedience.

I've made Abraham's 'Ishmael error' too many times in my own life. How about you? Are you forging an Ishmael in the furnace of your impatient heart and mind? Are you trying to force fulfilment? Are you allowing the longing for realization of a desire to push you outside the boundaries of faithful and trusting obedience to God? If you are doing any of these things, remember the lesson of Abraham. Remember that, while waiting is difficult, forcing things can be disastrous. Abraham's life warns us against trying to force fulfilment in our own way while we wait for the promises of God.

Why does God make us wait?

As we've seen, Abraham's life teaches us that we should deal with waiting by being faithful to God and by not forcing fulfilment. While we wait for fulfilment we need to trust in God and not in ourselves.

But perhaps you are wondering why God makes us wait for things? Why did he postpone fulfilment in the life of Abraham? Why does he postpone fulfilment in our lives? Why does he make us wait?

The best answers I have found to this 'why' question come from a seventeenth-century Dutch Puritan named Wilhelmus a Brakel. Brakel suggests the following six reasons why God postpones fulfilment in our lives:

> 1. *To prepare us for fulfilment:* 'One is not always capable of receiving the promised matter; rather, the Lord by way of postponement prepares the soul to be able to receive and make use of the promised matter properly. Similarly, one first cleanses and prepares a vessel before putting a delightful beverage in it, so that it will not leak out of a crack or assimilate the peculiar taste of the vessel.'

2. *To teach us to trust in him*: 'Postponement teaches one to believe without seeing and to acknowledge God as being truthful, even though He does not fulfil the promise as yet.'

3. *To remind us of his sovereignty*: 'Postponement teaches one to know and acknowledge God as being sovereign and only wise, who makes all things beautiful in His time.'

4. *To humble us:* 'Postponement will humble you, causing you to see your unworthiness and to understand that God will not give it to you for your sake.'

5. *To teach us to fear him*: 'Postponement causes one to fear for the Lord; it causes one to wait, to be quiet, and to be content with the present.'

6. *To increase our gratitude to him*: 'Postponement makes the soul more grateful when the desired matter arrives, causing the soul to rejoice all the more and to preserve it more carefully.'[3]

To summarize, God makes us wait for our good and his glory.

Abraham saw his day

But I would add a seventh reason to Brakel's list — God makes us wait so that we will fix our eyes on Jesus. Waiting for fulfilment displays to us our need of a Saviour. It is in the gap between promise and fulfilment that we learn of the inadequacy of our own faith and our need of a deliverer. It is in the waiting that we see the full extent of our spiritual disabilities. Waiting reveals to us that we are unable to journey from promise to fulfilment on our own — we need a Saviour.

Jesus is the pre-eminent example of one who faithfully waited on the promises of God. He waited faithfully through his life of humiliation, even through the cross, to receive his promised exaltation to the Father's right hand (Philippians 2:5-11). He never forced the Father's plan or attempted to impose his own will. When Satan tempted Jesus with an alternative plan to inherit the kingdoms of the world, Jesus unequivocally refused to create an Ishmael (Matthew 4:8-9). Unlike Abraham, Jesus never wavered from the will of God. This is why the writer to the Hebrews, after mentioning all the faithful saints in history in Hebrews 11, turns his readers' attention to Jesus, not only as the ultimate example of persevering and patient faithfulness, but also as the one who authors and perfects our own faith as we endure the challenges of waiting for the end of the age and the fulfilment of all of God's promises:

> Let us fix our eyes on Jesus, the author and perfecter of our faith, who for the joy set before him endured the cross, scorning its shame, and sat down at the right hand of the throne of God. Consider him who endured such opposition from sinful men, so that you will not grow weary and lose heart
>
> (Hebrews 12:2-3).

Our struggles with waiting and postponement should lead us to fix our eyes on Jesus.

Abraham's life is a tale about waiting. His life teaches us lessons, both positive and negative, regarding how to deal with waiting for the promises of God. But most of all Abraham's life serves as a road map directing us to Jesus Christ. It is through Jesus, the author and perfecter of our faith, that we are able to traverse the yawning gap between promises and fulfilment. Even Abraham understood this reality. He knew he needed a

Saviour. He was ultimately waiting for Jesus — his most glorious descendant (Galatians 3:16). Jesus testifies to this reality in his comments to the Pharisees in John 8:

> Your father Abraham rejoiced at the thought of seeing my day; he saw it and was glad
>
> (John 8:56).

If you really want to deal with waiting simply look to the one that Abraham saw, the one who authors and perfects your faith.

2.

What happened to Joseph:
dealing with forsakenness

So when Joseph came to his brothers, they stripped him of his robe
— the richly ornamented robe he was wearing — and they took
him and threw him into the cistern. Now the cistern was empty;
there was no water in it ... Judah said to his brothers, 'What will
we gain if we kill our brother and cover up his blood? Come, let's
sell him to the Ishmaelites and not lay our hands on him; after all,
he is our brother, our own flesh and blood.' His brothers agreed. So
when the Midianite merchants came by, his brothers pulled Joseph
up out of the cistern and sold him for twenty shekels of silver to the
Ishmaelites, who took him to Egypt
(Genesis 37:23-24, 26-28).

When his master heard the story his wife told him, saying, 'This is
how your slave treated me,' he burned with anger. Joseph's master
took him and put him in prison, the place where the king's prisoners
were confined
(Genesis 39:19-20).

The chief cupbearer, however, did not remember Joseph; he forgot him
(Genesis 40:23).

One of my favourite novels is Alexander Dumas' *The Count of Monte Cristo*. The novel tells the story of Edmond Dantes who is framed and sent away to rot in France's version of the notorious Alcatraz. Edmond is betrayed and forsaken.

In prison, Edmond spends the length of his days plotting how to escape and preparing for his ultimate revenge. After his escape, Edmond proceeds to painstakingly exact revenge on all who betrayed and forsook him. It is quite a colourful, adventurous and intriguing tale.

I've frequently questioned myself regarding why I like this novel so much. I ask myself: 'Why does this story of revenge resonate so much with me?' After all, it seems like a very 'unchristian' story! I think I have to admit that the reason I like this story is the very fact that it is about revenge, particularly revenge for being betrayed and forsaken by others.

On a very personal and visceral level, I find being forsaken one of the most painful human experiences and I enjoy *The Count of Monte Cristo* because the people who exacted this pain on Edmond are made to pay for it. For me it is a story about justice.

Being forsaken is a tremendously painful experience. Perhaps you have felt its sting in your own life. Maybe you have been forsaken by someone close to you, like a parent, child, spouse, friend, or even your church. Or maybe you have been forsaken by someone or something more distant, like a colleague, co-worker, employer or institution. It is likely that all of us will experience the pain of forsakenness sometime in our life. It is part of the human experience. It is part of the Christian experience. The question for us is how we will deal with it when it happens to us. How should a believer respond to being forsaken? Should we follow the example of Edmond Dantes or does Scripture call us to something else?

In this chapter we will explore how to deal with being forsaken by studying the life of the patriarch Joseph. Joseph understood the pain of forsakenness. He was forsaken by both his family and the world.

Forsaken by family

Bright beginnings

One could describe Joseph's early years as being charmed. He had a great deal going for him. He was indisputably his father's favourite son: 'Now Israel loved Joseph more than any of his other sons,' (Genesis 37:3). He also received a special garment, a 'richly ornamented' robe, as a token of his father's love (Genesis 37:3). This allowed everyone else to see how special he was and how much his father preferred him over his brothers. Finally, Joseph had a special gift. He received and could interpret special prophetic dreams.

But all of the things that made Joseph special also made him loathsome to his brothers. They were fiercely jealous and it is easy to understand why they felt this way. First, their father showed him obvious favouritism, particularly in giving him that special robe. Second, the dreams he received and interpreted were often quite self-serving. For example, in Genesis 37 we are told of two of Joseph's dreams which depict him in a position of superiority over his brothers (37:5-11). Joseph unwisely shared the content of these self-exalting dreams with his brothers. Given these factors, one can understand why his brothers hated him so and eventually an opportunity arose for them to exact their revenge against Joseph.

The conspiracy at Shechem

One day Joseph's brothers were out grazing the flocks near Shechem and Jacob decided to send Joseph to them to find out how they were doing. Joseph's brothers, who already possessed motive to seek revenge against him, now had the opportunity to do something about it. When they saw Joseph approaching from a distance they began to forge a conspiracy to kill him. They said to each other, 'Here comes that dreamer!' (Genesis 37:19). Reuben eventually talked his brothers out of killing Joseph. He convinced them to *only* throw him in a pit. In fact, Reuben secretly hoped to return later and rescue Joseph. When Joseph finally arrived they seized him, tore off his robe, and tossed him into a pit.

At this point, Judah, ever the scheming one, decided that it would be much more profitable to sell Joseph into slavery rather than leaving him to die. So Joseph's brothers sold him to some passing Ishmaelites for twenty shekels of silver, the going rate for a slave.

Now ponder for a moment the depth of the betrayal and treachery present in what Joseph's brothers did to him:

1. His own brothers, his own family, his own blood hated him. Three times in Genesis 37 we are told of how they despised him (Genesis 37:4, 5 & 8);
2. They hated him so much that they actually conspired to kill him;
3. They tore off his robe in order to shame and belittle him;
4. They discarded him like garbage in a pit;
5. When they realized that leaving him for dead had no profit in it, they decided to sell their own brother as a slave to a foreign enemy;
6. And if all this wasn't enough, they dipped his robe in blood, gave it to their father, and allowed him to believe that Joseph had been killed by animals.

Joseph had been utterly forsaken by his brothers.

There is nothing more painful in this world than being forsaken by someone you love. Just ask a spouse who has been abandoned by their partner, a child who has been abandoned by a parent, or someone who has been abused, manipulated or mistreated by someone they trusted. Perhaps you have experienced this pain in your own life. Joseph experienced it in his life. He was forsaken by his own family.

Forsaken by the world

Unfortunately for Joseph, this wasn't the only time that he experienced forsakenness in his life. Scripture records two additional instances where Joseph was forsaken. In these two instances it wasn't his family who forsook him, but rather he was forsaken by acquaintances, people he worked with, people who were not from his home and who did not share his religious beliefs and his ethnicity. In these instances, Joseph was forsaken by the world.

Joseph forsaken by Potiphar (and his wife!)

After Joseph was sold into slavery by his brothers he finds himself serving in the house of Potiphar, a high-ranking Egyptian official. Joseph excels as a slave and is promoted to Potiphar's second-in-command. But then, just when he's on top of the world again, Joseph draws the interest of his master's wife.

Joseph attempts to resist her advances, but she is relentless. One day, when all the other servants were out of the house, she cornered Joseph and he again rejected her. He ran off, but as he did, his garment was torn from his body (Genesis 39:11-12). Once again Joseph experienced the shame of being disrobed.

Potiphar's wife, spurned and vengeful, kept the garment and used it to falsely accuse Joseph of seducing her. When Potiphar learned of this he became angry and had Joseph imprisoned for a crime he did not commit. Joseph, who so loyally served his master, once again experienced the pain of being forsaken.

Joseph forsaken by the cupbearer

After Joseph enters prison he does what he always does, he experiences success and rises to the top. The warden of the prison makes Joseph his right-hand man. Joseph is put in charge of all the prisoners and all the administrative functions of the prison (Genesis 39:21-23).

While in prison, Joseph befriends two of Pharaoh's former servants, the cupbearer and the baker. One day, when Joseph encounters his new friends, they are very upset because the night before they had had dreams they could not understand. Joseph, of course, was gifted in interpreting dreams and so he generously offers his services. He interprets the dream of the cupbearer and tells him that his dream means that he will be restored to his position serving Pharaoh.

The cupbearer is obviously elated and grateful for this news, so Joseph makes one request of him: 'But when all goes well with you, remember me and show me kindness; mention me to Pharaoh and get me out of this prison' (Genesis 40:14). But the cupbearer did not keep his word and Genesis 40 concludes with these painful words: 'The chief cupbearer, however, did not remember Joseph; he forgot him,' (v. 23). Joseph had been forsaken a third time.

While being forsaken by someone you love is the most painful form of forsakenness, begin forsaken by employers, peers and friends is also painful. It is not easy to be forsaken by the world. It is hurtful to have someone in school purposely leave you out of some social event, group or activity. It is injurious to have a co-worker undercut you to secure a promotion at work. It is wounding to have an employer throw you aside like mere property in a corporate downsizing. Perhaps you have experienced this type of pain in your own life. Joseph experienced it in his life. He was forsaken by the world.

Dealing with forsakenness: learning from the example of Joseph

As we have seen, Joseph was a man who understood what it was like to be left behind, disregarded, forgotten, abandoned, exiled and forsaken. He was forsaken by his family and the world. He was forsaken by his Hebrew brothers, and his Gentile master and friends.

Just like us, Joseph understood the pain of being forsaken, but what is so remarkable is not that he experienced it, but rather how he responded to it and dealt with it. So let's look at how Joseph dealt with being forsaken and see what we can learn from him.

Our common responses to forsakenness

Before we begin our examination of how Joseph dealt with forsakenness, it is worth pausing for a moment to contemplate how we often deal with it. What are our usual responses to being forsaken? I think we generally respond to experiences of forsakenness in two ways.

The first common response is *The Count of Monte Cristo* response. We often seek revenge against those who forsook us. The second common response is to become bitter toward those who forsook us, and with God whom we blame for allowing us to be forsaken. Our response after being forsaken is not to serve and worship God, but rather it is frequently to despise him and become embittered toward him. We say to God, 'How could you let this happen to me?'

Don't you often find that you respond in these ways when you are forsaken? I know I am prone to such responses. But Joseph responded to being forsaken in a very different way and I believe in his response we find the biblical and Christian response to being forsaken. So let's now turn to how Joseph dealt with being forsaken.

Joseph's uncommon response to forsakenness

We can decipher Joseph's method of dealing with forsakenness by looking back at the three episodes of forsakenness in his life and noting what he did, and did *not* do, in response to them.

Episode 1: Forsaken by his brothers

How does Joseph respond to his brothers' brutal actions? He responded by serving God and others. He serves dutifully in Potiphar's house, so dutifully that he becomes the best slave he can be and is promoted to the highest level possible. But notice what is absent in his response. There is absolutely no sign of bitterness toward God or desire for revenge toward his brothers.

Episode 2: Forsaken by Potiphar

How does Joseph respond to Potiphar's cruelty? Once again he serves God and others. After being made a prisoner, even though he was innocent, Joseph becomes the best prisoner he can be. He's so faithful that he is promoted to the highest position possible for a prisoner. He also helps others. He interprets the dreams of his fellow prisoner the cupbearer and helps him to be restored to his position. But notice what is absent in his response. There is no sign of bitterness toward God or desire for revenge against Potiphar.

Episode 3: Forsaken by the cupbearer

How does Joseph respond to the callous forgetfulness of the cupbearer? He again serves God and others. When he leaves the prison he serves Pharaoh so faithfully that he becomes Pharaoh's second-in-command. But notice what is absent in his response. There is no sign of bitterness toward God or desire for revenge against the cupbearer.

Even more amazingly, after Joseph becomes second-in-command to Pharaoh his brothers come to Egypt seeking food for famished Israel. Joseph finds himself with an ideal opportunity to exact revenge against them. This moment is the inverse of Shechem where they betrayed him. But when his brothers come to him, Joseph does not seek revenge. He does teach them about the nature of their sin against him and he seeks their repentance; but he does not seek revenge. Joseph displays absolutely no evidence of bitterness toward his brothers or toward God. For example, note the generous spirit of Joseph in these remarks to his brothers after they came to Egypt seeking food:

'And now, do not be distressed and do not be angry with yourselves for selling me here, because it was to save lives that God sent me ahead of you. For two years now there has been famine in the land, and for the next five years there will not be ploughing and reaping. But God sent me ahead of you to preserve for you a remnant on earth and to save your lives by a great deliverance. So then, it was not you who sent me here, but God. He made me father to Pharaoh, lord of his entire household and ruler of all Egypt'
(Genesis 45:5-8).

Clearly, Joseph was no Edmond Dantes. His response to forsakenness and betrayal was not a response of bitterness and revenge. Instead, after each episode of forsakenness he faithfully served God and others wherever God put him.

Joseph reminds me of the hymn-writer Horatio Spafford. In 1873, Spafford lost his four daughters in a tragic shipping accident. Only his wife survived. During his voyage to meet his grieving wife, Spafford retired to his cabin and penned the words which would eventually become the beloved hymn 'It is well with my soul.' The hymn begins with these words:

When peace, like a river, attendeth my way,
When sorrows like sea billows roll;
Whatever my lot, Thou hast taught me to say,
It is well, it is well with my soul.

Like Spafford, Joseph responded to his forsakenness by saying, 'It is well, it is well with my soul.'

The one forsaken for us

Joseph shows us how to deal biblically with forsakenness. He calls us to serve God and others wherever God places us — be it in a pit, in servitude, or in a prison. But Joseph does one more thing that helps us to deal with forsakenness in our lives — he points us to Jesus, the one who was forsaken for us.

Consider the many similarities between Joseph and Jesus. Both are favourite sons of their fathers, both were hated by their brothers, both were conspired against, both had to resist temptation, both were stripped of their garments and both experienced forsakenness. Joseph was forsaken by his brothers, Potiphar and the cupbearer. Jesus was forsaken by his family, his disciples, his people, and the entire Gentile world. Of course, Jesus also experienced a unique form of forsakenness as part of his calling. He experienced being forsaken by his Father as a necessary consequence of becoming the sin-bearing Lamb of God: 'And at the ninth hour Jesus cried out in a loud voice, *"Eloi, Eloi, lama sabachthani?"* — which means, "My God, my God, why have you forsaken me?"' (Mark 15:34). This was the ultimate experience of forsakenness and it was experienced to glorify God and to redeem us. Jesus was forsaken for us.

Joseph's greatest function in the Bible is not ultimately to teach us how to respond to forsakenness, but rather to point us to the one who was forsaken for us. For Jesus not only promises to heal us of own personal experiences of forsakenness, betrayal and abandonment, but, more wonderfully, he promises that we will never experience what he experienced. Because Jesus was forsaken for us, we will never be spiritually abandoned, enslaved or imprisoned. We will never walk alone. We will never be forsaken. Jesus declares at the end of the Great Commission: 'And surely I am with you always, to the very end of the age', (Matthew 28:20).

The most extraordinary thing is that, even if we forsake him he will not forsake us. There is a wonderful illustration of this type of forgiveness in Joseph's life. As you will recall, Joseph's brothers stripped him of his special garment, but after Joseph restores his brothers Scripture records this act of Joseph: 'To each of them [his brothers] he gave new clothing, but to Benjamin he gave three hundred shekels of silver and five sets of clothes' (Genesis 45:22). In an act of forgiveness and compassion, Joseph, who had been stripped by his brothers, now gives them new garments. This is exactly what Jesus does for us. He takes our filthy, sin-drenched garments and gives us his robe of righteousness.

Joseph's greatest function in the Bible is not ... to teach us how to respond to forsakenness, but ... to point us to the one who was forsaken for us.

Get a grip!

Just like Joseph did with his brothers when they came to Egypt looking for food, Jesus will show us our sin and he will call us to repentance, but he will *not* seek revenge against us and he will never forsake us: 'Never will I leave you; never will I forsake you,' (Hebrews 13:5).

3.

What happened to Moses:

dealing with failure

One day, after Moses had grown up, he went out to where his own people were and watched them at their hard labour. He saw an Egyptian beating a Hebrew, one of his own people. Glancing this way and that and seeing no one, he killed the Egyptian and hid him in the sand. The next day he went out and saw two Hebrews fighting. He asked the one in the wrong, 'Why are you hitting your fellow Hebrew?' The man said, 'Who made you ruler and judge over us? Are you thinking of killing me as you killed the Egyptian?' Then Moses was afraid and thought, 'What I did must have become known.' When Pharaoh heard of this, he tried to kill Moses, but Moses fled from Pharaoh and went to live in Midian, where he sat down by a well
(Exodus 2:11-15).

Forty is an important number in our culture. Although there's a popular phrase that 'Fifty is the new forty,' the 'big four-o' is still an important age. I say this as one who will reach that milestone very soon. Because I am quickly approaching this milestone, I've been giving a lot of thought to the importance of forty years. Why does this age carry such significance? I can think of a couple of reasons.

First, I think forty carries such great significance because it's the age when we really finally reach maturity. It's an age that provides us with enough history to be able to gain some perspective on our lives. We see more clearly our own weakness, frailty and failures. We can assess more soberly what is really valuable in life.

I think the age of forty is also significant because it serves as a pivotal point in our lives. By the time we reach the age of forty we have inevitably encountered disappointment and failure in life. Perhaps this comes in the form of an unfulfilled dream, an unhappy marriage, or an unremarkable career. At the age of forty we are forced to confront the disappointments of our lives and determine whether we will allow them to dominate and control the remainder of our lives. We will either choose to live out our days embittered, thinking about what could have been, or we will choose to live out our days enlivened by the prospect of what could still yet be. I think that's the significance of the age of forty.

> We will either choose to live out our days embittered … or we will choose to live out our days enlivened by the prospect of what could still yet be.

Interestingly, forty is an important number in the life of Moses. Moses' life can be broken down into three main sections, each of which is demarcated by forty years of his life. In other words, Moses' life is a tale of three forties. When we look at Moses' life I think we find in it a story similar to our own. I think we find in it encouragement and instruction for dealing with the disappointments and failures experienced in our own lives. So let's trek through the 'three forties' of Moses' life and see what they teach us about dealing with failure.

The first forty years

The promise of Moses' early life

The first forty years of Moses' life began with great promise and privilege. From the day of his birth it was clear that Moses was special. Exodus 2:2 notes that when Moses' mother first glanced at him she 'saw that he was a fine child.' In Acts 7, Stephen recounts the history of Israel and he notes this about Moses: 'At that time Moses was born, and he was no ordinary child,' (Acts 7:20). Clearly, there was something special about Moses and it was evident from the day he was born.

Moses also had the privilege of being raised in a believing household by faithful parents. We can see the faith and courage of his parents in how they preserved Moses' life even in the face of the threats of Pharaoh. Just before Moses' birth, Pharaoh became fearful of the fruitfulness of the Israelites and so he gave an order to kill all the male Israelite babies. But Moses' mother was a faithful woman and she hid Moses for three months in order to protect him. When she could hide him no longer she devised a plan to safeguard him by placing him in a tiny ark and sending him afloat in the Nile.

Pharaoh's daughter spotted Moses in the river and adopted him as her own child. She even hired Moses' mother to be his nurse. Moses was saved by the courageous actions of his faithful parents. The writer to the Hebrews pays tribute to Moses' parents by declaring: 'By faith Moses' parents hid him for three months after he was born, because they saw he was no ordinary child, and they were not afraid of the king's edict,' (Hebrews 11:23).

Finally, Moses also had the benefit of a privileged upbringing and education. He was raised, trained and educated in Pharaoh's house. Stephen notes this privileged aspect of Moses' youth in Acts 7:22: 'Moses was educated in all the wisdom of the Egyptians and was powerful in speech and action.'

Moses had much going for him during the first forty years of his life. He was a special child, he had faithful parents and he received a first-class education. But despite having all of these advantages, Moses experienced a major failure just when it seemed like he was about to blossom.

Moses' failure

It is clear that during his first forty years Moses had become aware of his Hebrew ethnicity and perhaps even had some sense of his calling to protect, defend and deliver his people. For example, in Exodus 2:11-12 we learn that Moses understood that the Hebrews were 'his own people' and that he became outraged when he was witness to an Egyptian beating a fellow Hebrew. Understandably, Moses responded to this event by intervening, killing the Egyptian and delivering the Hebrew. However, it is this event which marks his early life failure.

Now at first glance one might look at this event and question why I would refer to it as a failure on Moses' part. After all, Moses was trying to correct an injustice. In fact, he even receives seeming approval and praise for this act in the New Testament (see Acts 7:25 and Hebrews 11:24-26). But it is also clear that Moses knew that he had done something wrong. For example, before killing the Egyptian, Moses glanced 'this way and that' to make sure no one saw his actions, and he hid the Egyptian's body in the sand in an attempt to cover his crime (Exodus 2:12). He also felt the pangs of a guilty conscience and the onset of shame when a fellow Hebrew later confronted him about this event: 'Are you thinking of killing me as you killed the Egyptian?' (Exodus 2:14).

But the main reason this event represents such a massive failure in Moses' life is that Moses tried to accomplish God's plan of delivering the Hebrew people in his own way and according to his own timetable. God would indeed one day call Moses to deliver Israel from bondage, but Moses jumps the gun here and he suffers for it. Instead of delivering God's people, he has to flee to the wilderness. Moses' promising life had spawned a great failure.

A warning for us

This failure of Moses should lead us to some self-examination regarding our own lives. For we too are prone to making similar mistakes, aren't we? We too often attempt to take control of God's plan and we inevitably discover ourselves mired in failure.

Like Moses, I know that I am often guilty of impatience when it comes to what I think God has called me to do. I too often slay the Egyptian in my life. How about you? Are you making the same mistake as Moses? Are you trying to force God's timing?

The second forty years

Wasted years?

As a result of his failure, Moses spent the middle part of his life, his second forty years, seemingly wasting away in the desert. During this second forty-year stretch Moses faced several discouraging realities. First, he entered the desert as a failure and a fugitive. He no longer possessed the privileges of Pharaoh's house. He had no money, was unemployed and running from the law. Second, he experienced a profound sense of alienation. For instance, note what Moses proclaimed at the birth of his son: 'Zipporah gave birth to a son, and Moses named him Gershom, saying, "I have become an alien in a foreign land,"' (Exodus 2:22). Finally, Moses was forced to work below his skill level during these years. He went from being a son in Pharaoh's

47

house and prospective deliverer of the Hebrew people to being a lowly shepherd in the desert (Exodus 3:1).

One cannot help but think that these years in the desert must have seemed like an utter waste of time to Moses. But in reality, God used these forty years, what could be called Moses' 'mid-life crisis', to shape him into a more useful instrument to achieve God's plans for him.

How did these discouraging realities shape Moses into a more useful instrument? First, they filled Moses with empathy for his people. Moses had grown up in privilege, but now he was forced to experience firsthand the pain of bondage and alienation which his brethren endured in Egypt. Second, these realities also served to humble him. In his youth, Moses was a 'golden boy' with everything going for him. Moses was not lacking in self-confidence. So God had to humble him; and he did it by sending him to the far side of the desert. It worked. Later we hear this astounding testimony of the depth of Moses' humility: 'Now Moses was a very humble man, more humble than anyone else on the face of the earth,' (Numbers 12:3).

A desert of fruitfulness

Moses' forty years in the desert teaches us that seeming failure can lead to real growth. Perhaps you have experienced failure recently. Maybe you experienced it in your job, as a parent, as a child, in school, as a spouse, as a Christian. Maybe you feel like you are a stranger in a foreign land, serving on the far side of the desert. Maybe you find this time depressing and discouraging. It is easy to become despondent at times like these.

Instead of becoming discouraged, however, perhaps we should ask ourselves: 'How is God using my failure in my life? What is he teaching me? What should I be learning? How will this failure help me to be more useful to God and to others?' Remember, some of God's best-used servants spent time in the desert — Moses, Paul and, of course, even our Lord. Moses' life reminds us that sometimes the far side of the desert can be the most fruitful place in which we can find ourselves.

The third forty years

In the last third of his life, Moses emerged from the desert and experienced great success. God used Moses as the human instrument to deliver his people out of bondage to Egypt. God also made Moses the mediator of his covenant. He became the liaison between God and his people. In this role, Moses had the privilege of communicating God's covenant to Israel. What a far cry from his days in the desert! Moses' life had truly come full circle. He had journeyed from failure to recovery.

Dealing with failure: lessons from the life of Moses

So what should we learn from the full pattern of Moses' life? I think the life of Moses teaches us two encouraging lessons which are applicable to our own lives. Moses teaches us that momentary spiritual failure does not exclude us from having long-term spiritual success; and that our spiritual success is not found in ourselves and our own performance.

Lesson 1: Our failures are only temporary

Many successful people in our world have experienced significant failures in their lives. J. K. Rowling's highly successful Harry Potter book about a boy wizard was initially rejected by twelve publishers. The Beatles were turned down by Decca Records which stated that they didn't 'like their sound'. Basketball great Michael Jordan was dropped from his high-school varsity basketball team in his second year. In his youth, G. K. Chesterton was informed by a teacher that if his head were opened 'we should not find any brain but only a lump of white fat.'[1]

Each of these examples serves as a reminder that *a* failure does not mean that we *are* failures. Each of these successful individuals recovered from an early failure in life. They went on to do great things in the eyes of the world. A similar dynamic often operates in our spiritual lives as we attempt to serve God in this world. The life of Moses displays this truth. Like J. K. Rowling, The Beatles, Michael Jordan and G. K. Chesterton, Moses, too, experienced failure early in his life only to go on to achieve great things.

The life of Moses reminds us that every believer will experience failure in his or her walk with God. Setbacks are inevitable as we continue to wrestle with sin. The road to glory is not a straight incline, but rather it is riddled with cliffs, curves, hills, valleys and detours.

> For the Christian failure is never a place of permanent residence, but rather it is only a temporary abode.

The life of Moses encourages us by demonstrating that sinful failures are never the end of the story for Christians. Even momentarily denying Jesus, as we learn from Peter's life, does not result in utter failure for the believer. Like Moses, Peter recovered from his failure, to serve the Lord in mighty ways. The point is that, for the Christian, failure is never a place of permanent residence, but rather it is only a temporary abode.

Lesson 2: Our success is found in Jesus

The pattern of Moses' life also teaches us that our success is found only in Jesus. His life reveals to us that only Jesus can make up for our failures and empower us to experience spiritual success. We see this through the comparisons and contrasts which we can draw between his life and the life of Jesus.

There are many comparisons between Moses and Jesus. Both were born when Israel was under bondage. Both were condemned to death by decrees of Gentile rulers. Both were miraculously delivered from death during their infancy by the faithful actions of their parents. Both found refuge by dwelling in Egypt for a time. Both fasted for forty days and forty nights in the wilderness. Both expounded God's law to God's people. Finally, both were mediators of God's covenant.

Clearly, there are many comparisons which can be drawn between Moses and Jesus. Each of these comparisons is meant to draw our attention to Jesus. But it is really through the contrasts between Moses and Jesus that we learn the lesson that our success can only be found in Jesus.

Jesus: a greater deliverer

First, consider what we learn from the contrast between Moses and Jesus in their work as deliverers of God's people. Whereas Moses *temporarily* delivered God's people out of the bondage of foreign oppression and human slavery, Jesus *permanently* delivered his people out of bondage to sin. Jesus is a greater deliverer than Moses and this reminds us that only Jesus can save us permanently from our failures. Only Jesus can free us from the dominion of sin and empower us to live godly lives.

Jesus: a greater mediator

An even more glorious contrast between Moses and Jesus is found by looking at their work as mediators. A mediator is one who stands between two parties and attempts to achieve reconciliation between them. Moses served in this role in the old covenant. He tried to reconcile God and his people Israel.

For me, Moses' shining moment, the greatest success of his life, occurred as he tried to fulfil this role of mediator in the aftermath of the incident with the golden calf which is recorded in Exodus 32.

As you will recall, that episode began with Moses descending from Mount Sinai after receiving the Ten Commandments, only to find God's people worshipping a golden calf. The people were violating the very commandments Moses had just been given. God was rightly angry over this sin and sought to destroy Israel, but Moses did something extraordinary. He interceded for his people and he declared the following to God: 'But now, please forgive their sin — but if not, then blot me out of the book you have written,' (Exodus 32:32).

What an amazing moment! Here we find Moses, once an incredible failure himself, offering himself to make up for the failures of God's people. But do you see Moses' problem? Moses couldn't do it. He couldn't give himself for the sins of others because he too was a sinner. But Jesus could do what Moses could not do. Jesus was able, and did, offer himself to make up for the failures of his people. Only Jesus can accomplish such a feat. Only Jesus can save us from our sins.

In Jesus there are no failures

The bad news is that because of Adam we are all born failures. We begin our lives in bondage. We begin our lives in need of recovery. We begin our lives in *Paradise Lost*. We only add to this inborn failure by own sinful actions. That's a depressing thought, isn't it? But that's not the end of the story.

The good news is that because of Jesus' work as our deliverer and mediator we are all reborn. We begin our new lives in Christ as those who have been liberated from the dominion of sin. We now live our lives in *Paradise Regained*.

Unfortunately, this doesn't mean that after our conversion our lives are entirely free from sin and failure. Even when we make progress, we will often fail by falling back into old patterns. Moses experienced this dynamic in his own life. After recovering from his early failure and experiencing incredible success, Moses experienced another failure at the very end of his life which resulted in him being denied the privilege of leading Israel into the promised land.

Moses' final failure is recorded for us in Numbers 20:7-13. In this account, God commanded Moses to bring forth water from a rock, but Moses forgot to honour and sanctify God before the people and God disciplined him: 'But the LORD said to Moses and Aaron, "Because you did not trust in me enough to honour me as holy in the sight of the Israelites, you will not bring this community into the land I give them"' (20:12). Moses lost the opportunity to lead Israel into the promised land.

Interestingly, after Moses' failure, it took a man named 'Joshua' to lead Israel into the promised land. The name 'Jesus' is a form of the Hebrew name 'Joshua.' Even Moses' final failure points us to Jesus. It took the new and greater 'Joshua' to lead Israel (the church) into the promised land of salvation. Moses could not bring his people there, but Jesus can and does! As the apostle John put it: 'For the law was given through Moses; grace and truth came through Jesus Christ,' (John 1:17).

As Moses' life demonstrates, we are flawed creatures even after our new birth. Failure is an inherent part of the Christian walk. Failure will always be with us in this world. But the life of Moses, and more importantly the work of Jesus, remind us that while we will continually experience failure in this world, we are *not* failures in the eyes of God. Because of Jesus and his glorious work on our behalf we are not sentenced to live out our days as miserable failures in the eyes of our Father. The Bible teaches us that Jesus' perfect life is imputed, or credited, to us. In other words, ultimately, when God the Father looks at our lives, he focuses not on our failures, but rather on the success of his beloved Son. Thus when we stand before God on the Day of Judgement our fate will not depend on the merits of our own deeds, but rather solely on the deeds of Jesus Christ. It is upon the merits of his successful life that our eternal destiny rests. That is *very* good news indeed!

If you are a follower of Jesus then you are no failure in the eyes of God. You have been recovered, redeemed and are in the process of being remade into the glorious image of Jesus Christ. Given this reality, isn't it time for you to move out of the far side of the desert and resume your journey to the promised land? Isn't it time that you moved from failure to recovery by placing your hope and trust solely in Jesus? Moses teaches us that the way to deal with failure is by looking to Jesus, the one who makes us perfect.

4.

What happened to Miriam:

dealing with jealousy

Miriam and Aaron began to talk against Moses because of his Cushite wife, for he had married a Cushite. 'Has the Lord *spoken only through Moses?' they asked. 'Hasn't he also spoken through us?' And the* Lord *heard this. (Now Moses was a very humble man, more humble than anyone else on the face of the earth.) At once the* Lord *said to Moses, Aaron and Miriam, 'Come out to the Tent of Meeting, all three of you.' So the three of them came out*
(Numbers 12:1-4).

William Penn, the Quaker leader and founder of the state of Pennsylvania, once wrote: 'The jealous are troublesome to others, but a torment to themselves.' Jealousy is a powerful human emotion. It opens the gateway to many different types of sins. Jealousy can spawn hatred, malice, gossip, envy, covetousness, rebellion and even murder.

But as the quote from William Penn indicates, jealousy not only harms the target of the jealousy, it also harms the source of the jealousy. As Penn rightly noted, people filled with jealousy are not only 'troublesome to others', they are also a 'torment to themselves'. With jealousy we not only destroy others, but we also run the risk of destroying ourselves.

The dually destructive nature of jealousy which Penn described can be witnessed in the life of Moses' sister Miriam. Although she was a great Old Testament saint, she was brought down by her own struggle with jealousy. The things that happened to Miriam can teach us lessons regarding the destructive power of jealousy and how to deal with it in our lives. Before we explore those lessons, let's look at the life of Miriam and get acquainted with the things that happened to her. We'll look at Miriam's life in three phases: the brave young girl, the strong mature woman and the jealous sister.

Miriam the brave young girl

The biblical record of Miriam's life begins with a description of an extraordinary act of bravery. We first hear about Miriam at the time of Moses' birth. At this time Miriam was a young girl between the ages of eleven and thirteen. Her younger brother Moses was in peril because of the decree of Pharaoh requiring the slaughter of all Hebrew male infants. Moses' mother devised a plan to preserve Moses' life. She placed him in a basket and set him adrift in the Nile hoping that he would be taken in by an Egyptian woman. But when Moses was set adrift by his mother he was not alone. The Scripture informs us that his sister Miriam was watching over him as he drifted down the Nile (Exodus 2:4).

Moses was eventually discovered by Pharaoh's daughter. Upon looking at Moses, Pharaoh's daughter declared: 'This is one of the Hebrew babies' (Exodus 2:6). At that exact moment, Miriam deftly thrust herself into the situation by suggesting the following plan to Pharaoh's daughter: 'Shall I go and get one of the Hebrew women to nurse the baby for you?' (2:7). Pharaoh's daughter agreed with Miriam's suggestion and Miriam rushed to get Moses' mother who became his nurse (2:8). Miriam's cleverness and self-sacrifice played a crucial role in preserving Moses' life. Her quick thinking also allowed Moses' godly mother to be a continuing influence on Moses' life. Because Miriam helped to preserve the life of Moses she was also used by God to advance the deliverance of God's people from Egypt. Her selfless act of bravery is even more extraordinary when we remember that she was a mere teenager at the time. Miriam's life begins with the actions of a brave young girl.

Miriam the strong mature woman

Miriam continued to play an important role in the history of Israel well into her adulthood. For example, during the period of Israel's exodus from Egypt Miriam served alongside her siblings Moses and Aaron as one of the leaders of Israel. In the prophecy of Micah, God attests to the leadership role of Miriam during the exodus: 'I brought you up out of Egypt and redeemed you from the land of slavery. I sent Moses to lead you, also Aaron and Miriam' (Micah 6:4).

Another sign of Miriam's significant role in Israel's history is the fact that she is the first woman in the Bible who is given the title 'prophetess' (Exodus 15:20). Her prophetic role emerges most notably in the period after the exodus when Israel celebrated its victory over the Egyptians by singing a song. The men were led in song by Moses and the women responded under the leadership of Miriam (15:20-21). Many biblical scholars believe that Miriam's song of response was an example of her prophetic role. In fact, some scholars contend that the entire song in Exodus 15 is attributable to Miriam's prophetic role.

As a mature woman of approximately ninety years of age, Miriam served Israel as a co-leader. She was a leader of the women of Israel. She was a prophetess. She played an integral role in the redemption of Israel.

Miriam the jealous sister

Unfortunately, like her brother Moses, Miriam's life ends on a tragic note. Her downfall occurred in the aftermath of the triumph of the exodus, just before Israel reached Mount Sinai. Her downfall was precipitated by the return of Moses' wife Zipporah.

Zipporah was the daughter of the priest Jethro. She was not a Hebrew. She was also a very strong-willed and powerful woman as evidenced by the episode in which she took charge and circumcised Moses' sons (Exodus 4:24-26). She had not been with Moses during the exodus, but she joined up with him as he was nearing Sinai.

Zipporah's return presented an immediate threat to Miriam's leadership role. Prior to Zipporah's arrival, Miriam was the undisputed leader among the women of Israel, but Zipporah's presence gave her a rival for this role. After all, Zipporah was the wife of Moses, daughter of a priest and a strong-willed woman. It would be natural for the women of Israel to look to her for leadership. Zipporah was the 'first lady' of Israel.

Zipporah's return also threatened Miriam's leadership because her father, Jethro, counselled Moses to spread the burden of leadership among seventy elders. Moses agreed to this and God blessed it by placing his Spirit upon these elders and allowing them to prophesy. But this expansion of the circle of Israel's leadership resulted in a diminished role for Miriam.

Miriam had been integral to the preservation of Moses' life as a child, she served alongside Moses and Aaron in the period of the exodus and she led the women in song; but now she found herself competing with Zipporah and seventy other men. She became jealous of Zipporah and Moses, and her jealousy fuelled a sinful response.

Miriam strikes out against Moses and Zipporah

In her jealousy, Miriam decided to strike a rebellious blow against Moses and Zipporah. She conspired with her brother Aaron, who was probably also jealous of Zipporah and the seventy elders. They decided to attack Moses for marrying a non-Israelite. Zipporah was a Cushite and this exposed Moses to a potential scandal. After all, the leader of Israel had married a non-Israelite, which was something Israelites were not supposed to do. Although Miriam had never raised this issue before, in the midst of her jealous rage she found an easy target and she pursued it with great zeal.

Although Aaron joined Miriam in this act of rebellion it is clear that Miriam was the ringleader. We know this because Miriam's name appears first in the account of the rebellion: '*Miriam* and Aaron began to talk against Moses because of his Cushite wife, for he had married a Cushite' (Numbers 12:1, emphasis mine). The order of names in the Bible is important and the name that appears first is generally the leader. For example, when God refers to the leadership of Israel in Micah 6:4 (the verse we saw earlier) the order of the names is as follows: Moses, Aaron and Miriam. This indicates that Moses was the primary leader of Israel. In the account of the rebellion, it is Miriam who takes the primary leadership role.

In Numbers 12:2, we see clearly that it was jealousy that provoked Miriam and Aaron. As they conspired together: "'Has the LORD spoken only through Moses?" they asked. "Hasn't he also spoken through us?"' In her jealousy, Miriam sought to undermine her brother and his wife. But someone else was taking note of the sinful discussion between Miriam and Aaron.

God punishes Miriam

The account of Numbers 12 indicates that God overheard the conversation between Miriam and Aaron. God was not pleased and he immediately responded by appearing at the tabernacle and summoning Moses, Aaron and Miriam to appear before him (12:4). There God appeared in a pillar of cloud and defended the authority of Moses. God declared the following regarding his special relationship with Moses: '*With him* I speak face to face, clearly and not in riddles; *he sees* the form of the LORD. Why then were you not afraid to speak against *my servant Moses?*' (12:8, emphasis mine).

The Bible makes it clear that God was very angry with both Miriam and Aaron (Numbers 12:9). Because of Miriam's sin of jealousy God punished her with leprosy (12:10). Aaron immediately intervened with Moses on Miriam's behalf:

> Please, my lord, do not hold against us the sin we have so foolishly committed. Do not let her be like a stillborn infant coming from its mother's womb with its flesh half eaten away (12:11-12).

Moses responded graciously to this plea for mercy by interceding with God on Miriam's behalf. Moses cried out to the Lord, 'O God, please heal her!' (12:13). God heard Moses' cry and reduced Miriam's sentence to that of being exiled from the camp for seven days (12:14). The Bible notes that Israel did not move during those seven days, but instead waited for the return of Miriam (12:15).

Miriam's jealousy led her to take foolish and sinful actions. Her jealousy marginalized her role in Israel's history and made her less useful to God. After her exile we hear little of Miriam's influence in the life of Israel. The next time we hear of her is at her death (20:1).

Lessons from the life of Miriam

When we look at the life of Miriam we see the destructive power of jealousy. The question for us is: what can we learn from Miriam's mistakes? The things that happened to Miriam have much to teach us about dealing with jealousy. Her life displays for us the impetus for dealing with jealousy because it shows us the great harm that can be caused by it. Her life also shows how to deal with jealousy when it arises in our lives. Here are three lessons from the life Miriam regarding dealing with jealousy.

Lesson 1: Jealousy opens a gateway to other sins

One of the lessons that can be learned from the things that happened to Miriam is that sinful jealousy frequently sparks a myriad of other sins. While jealousy is an internal emotion of the heart and mind, it can quickly spill over into external actions. In Miriam's case, the jealousy in her heart led her to engage in conspiracy and rebellion. Some biblical scholars also believe that Miriam's jealousy led her to embrace racial prejudice against Zipporah who, as a Cushite, had a darker complexion. The point is that when the sin of jealousy is entertained in the heart it is not long before it sparks other sins in our lives.

The fact that jealousy is a gateway to other sins is supported by other parts of the Bible. For example, Proverbs 6:34 reveals that jealousy in romantic relationships can lead to violence: 'for jealousy arouses a husband's fury, and he will show no mercy when he takes revenge'. In Acts 13:45 the apostle Paul's success stoked jealousy among the Jewish leaders and this led to

> When the sin of jealousy is entertained in the heart it is not long before it sparks other sins in our lives.

abusive speech: 'When the Jews saw the crowds, they were filled with jealousy and talked abusively against what Paul was saying.' In numerous passages in the New Testament Paul groups jealousy with a broader list of divisive types of sins like dissension, quarrelling, gossip, anger, arrogance, slander, selfish ambition, and fits of rage (Romans 13:13; 2 Corinthians 12:20; and Galatians 5:20). The grouping of jealousy with these other sins suggests an interrelationship among them. In other words, jealousy often produces dissension, quarrelling, gossip, anger, arrogance, slander, selfish ambition and fits of rage. This is exactly what happened to Miriam. Jealousy opened the door to other sins.

One of the lessons we learn from Miriam's life about dealing with jealousy is the importance of diffusing it in the heart before it is allowed to blossom into even more damaging actions. We simply cannot allow ourselves to indulge thoughts of jealousy because they will disable our moral compass and lead us into other sins. The sin of jealousy must not be trifled with because it is very powerful. Proverbs reminds us of its power by contending that it is even more powerful than anger and fury: 'Anger is cruel and fury overwhelming, but who can stand before jealousy?' (Proverbs 27:4).

When we detect the spark of jealousy emerging in our hearts the best course of action is to seek to extinguish it before it ignites into flames. We should seek the Lord in prayer at these times and pray that the Holy Spirit would mortify such thoughts within us. We must not allow jealousy to take root in our heart. If Miriam had only contained and neutered her jealousy she would not have allowed herself to engage in a prideful act of rebellion against Moses.

Lesson 2: Jealousy undermines the work of the church

The things that happened to Miriam also teach us that jealousy can be particularly destructive to the work of the church.

Miriam's jealousy not only impacted her own spiritual life and the life of Moses, but it also affected the congregation of God's people. Her jealousy undermined the work of the church in three ways.

First, Miriam's jealousy resulted in wasted time for Moses and Israel. Her jealousy led her to make an accusation against Moses and Zipporah. This accusation was an attempt to scandalize Moses and it required that he respond. Instead of leading Israel forward to the promised land, Moses was sidetracked by an unnecessary distraction. Her jealousy occupied the time of all three of Israel's leaders and it likely impacted the seventy elders as well. It was a colossal waste of time that diverted the church from the core of its ministry.

Second, Miriam's jealousy halted the spiritual progression of the entire church. Miriam's punishment for her jealousy placed her outside the camp for seven days. During this period of time the people of Israel remained stagnant. They did not move closer to the promised land. One jealous member of the body brought a stop to the spiritual progression of the entire church.

Third, Miriam's jealousy raised dissension and factionalism in the ranks of the church. She pitted her and Aaron's ministry against that of Moses. It is clear that Miriam was a leader in the eyes of many in Israel, particularly the women. Her actions likely stirred up her supporters and brought division. As we've seen from various New Testament passages, jealousy in the church often leads to factions and dissensions (Romans 13:13; 2 Corinthians 12:20; and Galatians 5:20). One thinks of the apostle Paul and the jealous factionalism he had to address in the church in Corinth when the members were following their favourite leader (1 Corinthians 1:12).

One of the lessons we learn from the life of Miriam is that jealousy can undermine the work of the church. Problems caused by jealousy can waste the time of church leadership, stagnate the progress of the entire body and lead to church divisions. The destructive consequences which result from personal jealousies remain a major problem for the modern church. How many pastors have been drawn away from ministry by having to attend to small-minded matters of personal jealousy in the congregation? How many congregations have lost opportunities to minister because their attention was drawn inward by a dispute sparked by jealousy? How many congregations have been fractured and torn by jealousy?

Lesson 3: Jealousy is ultimately self-destructive

The things that happened to Miriam have one additional lesson for us. We learn from Miriam's struggle with jealousy that while jealousy often leads us to seek to destroy the lives of other people, in the end jealousy ultimately results in self-destruction.

Miriam's jealousy was aimed at bringing down Moses and Zipporah, but the actions she took led to her own downfall. She sought to remove Moses from leadership, but it was she who was removed from leadership. If it was not for the intercession of Moses and the mercy of God, Miriam would have lost more than just her leadership role, she would have lost her life. There is a 'boomerang' effect to jealousy. It may lead us to strike out at others, but ultimately its destructive power comes back on us.

When we entertain personal jealousies and allow them to blossom into other sinful actions we are setting ourselves up for a bitter irony. Jealousy is a parasite which feeds on the sustenance of our souls. It contributes nothing to our well-being or the well-being of others. It simply extracts from us and its toll is heavy. Jealousy erodes our joy and robs us of the privilege of sharing in other people's accomplishments.

We see this self-destructive and parasitic impact of jealousy in the life of King Saul. Saul's jealousy of David ate at him continually. One example of this occurs in 1 Samuel 18 when Saul was still king and David was one of his military leaders. Israel had just won a great victory against their arch enemies the Philistines. When the armies of Israel returned home the people celebrated by singing: 'Saul has slain his thousands, *and David his tens of thousands*' (1 Samuel 18:7, emphasis mine). The Bible records Saul's jealous response to this in the very next verse: 'Saul was very angry; this refrain galled him. "They have credited David with tens of thousands," he thought, "but me with only thousands. What more can he get but the kingdom?"' (18:8).

Saul's jealousy led him to take a variety of sinful actions aimed at preventing David's ascendancy. Saul tried with all his might to hang on to his claim to kingship. But his efforts ultimately led to his own downfall. Saul's personal jealousy toward David consumed all that he did until it also finally consumed him. Just as with Miriam, Saul's jealousy ultimately proved self-destructive.

The things that happened to Miriam serve as a warning to us regarding the effects of jealousy on our own lives. The petty jealousies that exist within our sinful hearts are not our friends. They may first appear cloaked in the uniform of our allies, but they are in the end a great enemy in disguise. Our goal should be to eradicate our petty jealousies before we allow them to consume us. In order to do this, we need to seek the Lord in prayer and request the power of the Holy Spirit in our lives. Only the fruit of God's Spirit can overcome the bitter bile of jealousy.

> Only the fruit of God's Spirit can overcome the bitter bile of jealousy.

The merciful love of our jealous God

In this chapter we have spent a great deal of time exploring the wicked ramifications of jealousy in the human heart. This may lead you to believe that jealousy is always a sinful emotion, but that is not the case. After all, God himself is described as being 'a jealous God' (Exodus 20:5). God is jealous of our loyalty, affection and worship. God's jealousy is never sinful. There are even some rare times when human jealousy is appropriate. We can be jealous for the name and worship of God, we can be appropriately jealous of the affection and loyalty of our spouse and, like the apostle Paul, we can be jealous for the people of God (2 Corinthians 11:2).

But while God always maintains a holy jealousy, we humans rarely ever do. As we've seen in this chapter, most of the time in the human experience jealousy destroys relationships, hinders the work of the church and limits our own usefulness to the kingdom. Yet even though human jealousy is so universally destructive, it is very likely that everyone reading this book has given into its power at some time in their life and felt the sting of its wounds. Whether we like to admit it or not, we all struggle with jealousy.

The real hope we have to counter the destructive effects of jealousy in our lives, relationships and churches is to look to our jealous God for mercy. Miriam received healing and redemption for her sin of jealousy through the intercession of Moses with God. We need to deal with the sin of jealousy in the same way. We need to seek the high priestly intercession of Jesus at the throne of God's grace to find help and mercy for our time of need (Hebrews 4:14-16). In another great irony, it is only the God who describes himself as 'jealous' who can deliver us from the peril of jealousy in our own lives. We learn this lesson from the things that happened to Miriam.

5.

What happened to the two Tamars and Jephthah's daughter:

dealing with injustice

Judah recognized them and said, 'She is more righteous than I, since I wouldn't give her to my son Shelah.'
And he did not sleep with her again
(Genesis 38:26).

'My father,' she replied, 'you have given your word to the LORD. Do to me just as you promised, now that the LORD has avenged you of your enemies, the Ammonites'
(Judges 11:36).

He called his personal servant and said, 'Get this woman out of here and bolt the door after her.' So his servant put her out and bolted the door after her. She was wearing a richly ornamented robe, for this was the kind of garment the virgin daughters of the king wore. Tamar put ashes on her head and tore the ornamented robe she was wearing. She put her hand on her head and went away, weeping aloud as she went
(2 Samuel 13:17-19).

Get a grip!

Do you ever struggle with the question of why bad things happen to good people? I find it to be one of the most challenging questions posed by those who oppose the Christian faith. I also find it a challenging question on a personal level. As Christians, we believe in a benevolent and loving God who is all knowing and all powerful. Yet, when I behold the injustices which so frequently occur in this world I admit that I sometimes struggle to reconcile them with what I know of God's character. At first glance, it often seems incongruous to me that a just God would allow injustices to occur.

In 1981, Harold Kushner wrote a best-selling book entitled, *When Bad Things Happen to Good People*. In the book he wrestled with the apparent incongruity of a just God and an unjust world. He had personally experienced the extraordinarily painful, and seemingly unjust, loss of one of his children. In his book, Kushner resolved the perceived incongruity between belief in a just God and the existence of an unjust world by concluding that God must not be all powerful. In other words, Kushner argued that God isn't in control of the events which give rise to the injustices we see in our world. Kushner shielded God from having any role to play in such injustices.

But by shielding God in this manner, Kushner also reduced God into something less than the God of the Bible. He stripped God of his sovereignty and omnipotence. In my mind, Kushner's supposed cure is much worse than the disease. Kushner's solution leaves us with a God who is powerless over our circumstances. If we accept Kushner's logic we are left wondering whether God is really in control of anything. Can God really save us from sin and death? Does he know what will happen tomorrow? Kushner is just plain wrong.

But if Kushner is wrong, then we are still left with the problem of dealing with injustice. We have to wrestle with the question of how to make sense of it. We also have to struggle with the question of how we should respond to injustices in our lives.

These are very complex questions, but I think we find some answers to them in the lives of three Old Testament women who share the common bond of being victims of gross injustice. Bad things happened to these good women. In this chapter we will explore the injustices suffered by these women and we will see how the things that happened to them can be used to teach us how to deal with injustice in our own lives.

Injustice in the life of the Tamar of Genesis

Our first story of injustice comes from the life of Tamar, the daughter-in-law of the patriarch Judah. Her story is recorded in Genesis 38. Tamar was married to Er, Judah's eldest son, but Er died, leaving Tamar a widow. Tamar found herself without a husband and without a son. In the Old Testament world this put her in a very precarious position. But the Old Testament law protected women in Tamar's situation by allowing them to continue their husband's line through one of his brothers. So Tamar pursued her rights under the law and Judah commanded his son Onan to fulfil this obligation.

But Onan was not keen on the idea of producing a male heir for his deceased elder brother because this heir would be in competition with him for the family inheritance. So Onan refused to live up to his obligations under the law. God was not pleased with Onan. In fact, God considered this sin so grave that he took Onan's life in judgement. So Tamar remained in her precarious situation.

After Onan's death, Tamar visited Judah a second time seeking to convince him to give her another of his sons. But Judah was not responsive to her requests. He brushed off his responsibilities and ignored her pleas. He procrastinated. He refused to give Tamar another one of his sons. Why did Judah refuse? Perhaps he was simply being selfish, or perhaps he feared that Tamar was a cursed woman; after all, two of his sons had died in her company.

Whatever the reason for Judah's refusal, Tamar found herself in serious trouble. She had no means of supporting herself and she had been denied what was rightly hers under the law. She had suffered an injustice at the hands of Judah. But Tamar was a very clever and strong-willed woman. She was not about to let Judah get away with this injustice. She carefully devised a plan to obtain justice.

Tamar's plan involved disguising herself as a prostitute and enticing Judah to purchase her services. Judah took her up on her offer, but he did not have enough money to pay for her services. When Judah promised to pay her later, Tamar agreed; but she demanded that Judah post some collateral. Tamar requested Judah's seal and staff, as these would be irrefutable proof of his identity. In modern terms, having Judah's seal and staff was like having his fingerprints or DNA.

Tamar became pregnant from her encounter with Judah and she eventually revealed to him that he was the father of her child. At first Judah denied Tamar's claims and he even tried to have her killed, but then Tamar produced Judah's seal and staff as evidence of his paternity. There was no point in Judah denying it any longer. He acknowledged that the child was his and he confessed his guilt, and Tamar's innocence, by stating: 'She is more righteous than I, since I wouldn't give her to my son Shelah' (Genesis 38:26). After a long struggle, Tamar finally received justice.

Injustice in the life of Jephthah's daughter

Our second tale of injustice occurred at the time when Israel was ruled by various judges. It would be an understatement to say that this was not Israel's golden age. During the time of the judges Israel engaged in repeated cycles of unfaithfulness. These persistent failures contributed directly to the injustice suffered by Jephthah's daughter.

The story of the injustice suffered by Jephthah's daughter begins with her father. Jephthah was a brutish man with a chequered past. His introduction in Scripture states: 'His mother was a prostitute' (Judges 11:1). Because he was born from a Canaanite prostitute his brothers never accepted him. He was eventually banished from Israel because of his behaviour and his half-breed lineage. Jephthah lived alone in exile.

However, Jephthah did have one thing going for him — he was a mighty warrior. He knew how to wage war and at this time in Israel's history they were desperate for a military leader. Israel faced a significant military threat from the Ammonites and they had no general to lead their army. But instead of looking to God for wisdom and strength, Israel looked to Jephthah for muscle and might. Jephthah's half-brothers, who were now the elders of Israel, begged Jephthah to return and lead Israel into battle. Jephthah agreed.

Initially Jephthah attempted to negotiate peace with the Ammonites, but without success. After failing in these peace talks, Jephthah turned his attention to preparing himself and his troops for battle. During these preparations, he became filled with lust for victory. This led him to make a very unwise and rash vow to God which is recorded in Judges 11:30-31: 'If you give the Ammonites into my hands, whatever comes out of the door of my house to meet me when I return in triumph from the Ammonites will be the LORD's, and I will sacrifice it as a burnt offering.'

Jephthah ultimately proved victorious in battle and as he returned home from victory his daughter ran out to greet him. She came out dancing and rejoicing over Israel's victory, and to honour her father. But upon seeing his daughter, Jephthah's victory celebration came to an end. He was filled with despair because he remembered his vow. He tore his clothes in lamentation and blamed his daughter for his circumstances: 'When he saw her, he tore his clothes and cried, "Oh! My daughter! You have made me miserable and wretched, because I have made a vow to the LORD that I cannot break"'(Judges 11:35).

Jephthah made no effort to rescind his vow or find another solution to his dilemma. He never prayed about it. He never offered to substitute himself in his daughter's place. He never gave any thought to the fact that God abhors human sacrifice.

Jephthah's daughter did not try to run from this vow. She voluntarily affirmed its validity and submitted herself to it (11:36). Her only request was a two-month delay in carrying out the vow so that she could mourn the fact that she had never married and had no children. After the two months had expired, Scripture records that Jephthah kept his abhorrent vow.

Jephthah's daughter had done no wrong. She behaved in an exemplary fashion throughout her ordeal. Yet, she lost her life and her father faced no punishment for his foolishness. She died as a result of her father's rash vow. Jephthah's daughter suffered a grave injustice.

Injustice in the life of the Tamar of 2 Samuel

Our final account of injustice occurred in the life of a second woman named Tamar. This Tamar lived in the time of the Davidic kingdom. She was a daughter of David and a descendant of the Tamar of Genesis. In 2 Samuel 13 we learn that David's eldest son, Amnon, had become infatuated with his half-sister Tamar. The Bible states that Amnon 'fell in love' with Tamar (2 Samuel 13:1) and he quickly became 'frustrated' by his inability to have her (13:2).

Amnon, with the help of his friend Jonadab, hatched a scheme to entrap Tamar so that Amnon could act on his lust.

Their conspiracy involved Amnon pretending to be ill so he could lure Tamar into his house. Tamar was a kind and godly woman and when she heard of Amnon's illness she brought him food to help him recover. When Tamar arrived at Amnon's house, he dismissed all his servants and ordered them to leave the premises. He was now alone with Tamar and he commanded her: 'Bring the food here into my bedroom so I may eat from your hand,' (13:10).

When Tamar entered his bedroom to feed her half-brother, Amnon acted upon his lust in a brutal way: 'But when she took it to him to eat, he grabbed her and said, "Come to bed with me, my sister,"' (13:11). Tamar refused and attempted to resist Amnon's advances, but Amnon refused to take 'no' for an answer and he raped Tamar.

If this wasn't cruel enough, after Amnon abused Tamar physically he then proceeded to abuse her verbally as well: 'Then Amnon hated her with intense hatred. In fact, he hated her more than he had loved her. Amnon said to her, "Get up and get out!"' (13:15). Once Amnon had what he wanted he discarded Tamar like refuse.

Tamar was left sexually violated and emotionally wounded at the hands of her half-brother. She walked around the gates of the city with ashes on her head. She lived with the scars of this encounter for the rest of her life. She became a recluse and never married. In many respects, Tamar died that day at the hands of Amnon. Like the Tamar of Genesis and Jephthah's daughter, Tamar also suffered a great injustice.

Lessons from the lives of these three women

In this chapter we've explored the lives of three women and the injustices they endured. In each case, the women were exemplary in their godliness and righteousness. There is no indication whatsoever that they were the least bit complicit in the events that radically changed their lives, but, nonetheless, bad things happened to these good people.

We often witness, and sometimes experience, similar tales of injustice in our own day and in our own lives. Perhaps you are experiencing such an injustice right now. It is likely that the injustice you are experiencing is not as grave as the injustices experienced by these women, but even so it is difficult to suffer an injustice of any degree. The lives of these three women have much to teach us about dealing with injustice in our lives. Let's look at three lessons of how to deal with injustice which can be drawn from the things that happened to them.

Lesson 1: Sometimes we must actively seek redress for injustice

The account of the life of the Tamar of Genesis teaches us that sometimes we need to fight back against the perpetrators of injustice. Tamar went to extreme lengths to make certain that Judah fulfilled his obligations to her under God's law. While we might not be comfortable with how she obtained justice, the Scripture never condemns her for her aggressiveness. In fact, Scripture portrays her as a heroine of righteousness. Tamar's actions demonstrate that we are not always to turn the other cheek in the face of injustice.

However, it is important to keep Tamar's response in proper perspective. Tamar's resistance and the nature of her drastic response are justified because of the particular circumstances surrounding the injustice she suffered. The injustice perpetrated against Tamar by Judah not only threatened Tamar's personal welfare, but it put the entire covenant line of the Messiah at risk. For example, we learn from Matthew's Gospel that Tamar and her descendants would become part of the genealogy of Jesus (Matthew 1:3). In the unfathomable mystery of God's providence, the child that Tamar bore in her seemingly scandalous encounter with her father-in-law played an incredibly significant role in redemptive history.

Now not many of us will find ourselves in a situation like the one in which Tamar found herself. This does not mean, however, that we will never encounter a situation in which we too are called to actively redress an injustice. We must remember that Tamar was not acting solely for her own benefit, but rather she was acting for the benefit of her deceased husband. Tamar's husband was Judah's eldest son and thus entitled to his inheritance. This inheritance would have passed to the eldest son of Tamar's husband. Therefore, Judah's refusal to adhere to God's law by producing a male heir for his deceased son trampled upon his rights. But Tamar's husband had no way to redress this injustice and so Tamar did it for him.

I think the Bible is clear that we are permitted and called to defend the rights of others, particularly those who are unable to defend themselves. God calls us to promote justice for widows, orphans and strangers. God wants us to seek redress for injustice perpetrated against the powerless. This is exactly what Tamar was doing by defending the legacy of her deceased husband who could no longer advocate for himself.

> We are permitted and called to defend the rights of others, particularly those who are unable to defend themselves.

The things that happened to Tamar teach us that there are times when we should seek redress for injustice. We are to seek redress when the integrity of God's law is at stake and when we are defending the rights of the powerless.

Lesson 2: Sometimes we must passively suffer injustice

Jephthah's daughter teaches us a very different lesson from the one we learned from the Tamar of Genesis. Jephthah's daughter teaches us that sometimes we need to accept injustice and suffer for the sake of others. Unlike with Tamar, the injustice perpetrated against Jephthah's daughter directly impacted only her. It was only her life and her rights which were being violated. Furthermore, by choosing to suffer this injustice voluntarily she was actually benefiting and serving other people.

Jephthah's vow occurred because Israel was at the mercy of the Ammonites. The reason they were at the mercy of the Ammonites was because of their sinfulness. The book of Judges recounts a cyclical pattern in which Israel repeatedly fell into sin and this sinfulness resulted in God giving them over to their enemies (Judges 10:6-7). In accepting the consequences of her father's foolish vow, Jephthah's daughter willingly chose to suffer for the sake of her father's dignity and for the entire nation. We can witness her willingness to sacrifice herself for others in her comments to her father after he realized the dreadful consequences of his vow: "'My father,' she replied, "you have given your word to the LORD. Do to me just as you promised, now that the LORD has avenged you of your enemies, the Ammonites'" (Judges 11:36).

Jephthah's daughter did not protest this injustice. Instead she willingly and freely chose to endure it. In this way, Jephthah's daughter's actions foreshadow the work of Jesus who, although innocent, willingly chose to suffer an injustice to deliver his people from their sins. This is why the church father, Origen, viewed Jephthah's daughter as a martyr. He considered her death as resulting in the deliverance of the people of God. The redemptive view of the story of Jephthah's daughter also appears in a poem written about her by Lord Byron:

> Though the virgins of Salem lament,
> Be the judge and the hero unbent!
> I have won the great battle for thee,
> And my father and country are free!

When this blood of thy giving hath gushed,
When the voice that thou lovest is hushed,
Let my memory still be thy pride,
And forget not I smiled as I died!

Many feminist scholars have pointed to the account of Jephthah's daughter as an example of the Bible's denigration of women. They question why sons like Isaac (Genesis 22:1-19) and Jonathan (1 Samuel 14:24-46) were spared, but not Jephthah's daughter. They see her suffering as a meaningless random act of violence against women. While it is true that human history too often reveals a tolerance for abuse against women, the suffering of Jephthah's daughter was far from meaningless. It was redemptive. Jephthah's daughter willingly gave herself for others.

The things that happened to Jephthah's daughter teach us that as believers we are sometimes called to suffer injustice for the sake of others. When we do this we imitate the work and character of our Lord.

Lesson 3: Sometimes we must wait for justice

Finally, the life of the Tamar of 2 Samuel reminds us that sometimes we need to wait for someone else to redress an injustice for us. Tamar's injustice was redressed by the actions of her half-brother Absalom. When Absalom learned of the rape of Tamar he was enraged and plotted to kill Amnon. He eventually proved successful in carrying out his revenge (2 Samuel 13:28-29). While Tamar sought no vengeance or redress, God used Absalom as an instrument of justice against Amnon.

Sometimes when we suffer injustice we must wait for God to bring redress. Paul writes the following in his epistle to the Romans: 'Do not take revenge, my friends, but leave room for God's wrath, for it is written: "It is mine to avenge; I will repay," says the Lord' (Romans 12:19). God may redress these injustices during this age, like he did in Tamar's life, or he may postpone his vengeance until the return of Christ; but either way every injustice will be redressed by God.

Perhaps someone reading this book has experienced the terror and pain of sexual and physical abuse like that experienced by Tamar. While such wounds are deep and slow to heal, remember the life of Tamar and how she reminds us of the coming work of Jesus who will avenge every injustice. Jesus will set right every wrong. Sometimes we need to wait for justice.

The need for a better king

The lives of these three women teach us three different lessons about how to respond to injustice. While most of us, thankfully, will never experience injustice on the level suffered by these women, the lessons learned from their lives can nonetheless be applied to a vast array of injustices, including those we encounter in our own lives. Thus when you experience injustice in your life, or witness it in the lives of others, you can look to the lessons gleaned from these women and consider how they might apply to your particular situation. God's Word, and his wisdom, will help guide you in choosing the proper response.

While the lives of these three women teach us different ways to deal with injustice, there is one unifying thread that weaves their accounts together. A fourth lesson that emerges from their lives is the reality that we are in desperate need of a better king and a just judge.

Consider for a moment what unifies the stories of these three women. Each one suffered at the hand of a leader in Israel. The first Tamar suffered at the hand of Judah who was a patriarch and a leader of Israel. Jephthah's daughter suffered at the hand of her father who was a judge of Israel. The second Tamar suffered at the hands of Amnon, a prince and a potential heir to David's throne, and at the hands of her powerful father, King David, who did nothing to redress her injustice. Each of these women suffered injustice at the seat of power. The system of government failed them. The voices of these three women finds a common refrain: 'We need a better king!'

That better king, of course, is the Lord Jesus Christ. He is a King who understands the injustices which are so often meted out by human kings, having been a victim of such an injustice himself. Jesus was wrongly accused, convicted in a sham trial and executed as an innocent man. But King Jesus not only understands injustice, he will also redress every injustice ever perpetrated by man. The book of Revelation portrays Jesus as a king and a judge seated on a throne:

> King Jesus not only understands injustice, he will also redress every injustice ever perpetrated by man.

> Then I saw a great white throne and him who was seated on it. Earth and sky fled from his presence, and there was no place for them. And I saw the dead, great and small, standing before the throne, and books were opened. Another book was opened, which is the book of life. The dead were judged according to what they had done as recorded in the books
>
> (Revelation 20:11-12).

Revelation promises us that at the end of the age Jesus will render judgement on every action by man. For those whose names are written in the book of life, there will be no condemnation in this judgement (Romans 8:1), but for those who reject Jesus due process will be meticulously followed. In the end the books will be balanced and the scales of justice will be levelled.

But Revelation also has another promise for us. Not only will Jesus redress every injustice, he will also heal the hurts of the wronged and injured: 'He will wipe every tear from their eyes. There will be no more death or mourning or crying or pain, for the old order of things has passed away' (Revelation 21:4). On that great day, injustice will be no more. The two Tamars and Jephthah's daughter, and all those who have suffered injustice, will not only have their justice, but they will also have healing and peace.

Although we cannot fully answer the question of why bad things happen to good people, we know from the stories of these three women that one of the reasons is that there are sinful people in the world like Judah, Amnon, David, Jephthah and you and me. Sin explains the presence of evil and injustice in this world. But the good news is that Jesus vanquished sin through the cross. Through the cross good things happen to bad people like you and me. God gave Jesus the justice we should have received so that we could receive the mercy we did not deserve: 'God made him who had no sin to be sin for us, so that in him we might become the righteousness of God' (2 Corinthians 5:21). In the end, the best way for us to deal with injustice in our lives is to keep the cross ever before our eyes.

6.

What happened to Elijah:

dealing with fear

Now Ahab told Jezebel everything Elijah had done and how he had killed all the prophets with the sword. So Jezebel sent a messenger to Elijah to say, 'May the gods deal with me, be it ever so severely, if by this time tomorrow I do not make your life like that of one of them.' Elijah was afraid and ran for his life
(1 Kings 19:1-3).

When I was a teenager I enjoyed viewing a television programme called *ABC's Wide World of Sports*. I was particularly enamoured with the introduction to the programme during which the narrator would say, 'Spanning the globe to bring you the constant variety of sport ... the thrill of victory ... and the agony of defeat ... the human drama of athletic competition... This is *ABC's Wide World of Sports!*' During the phrase 'agony of defeat' they would display film footage of a devastating crash by a ski jumper. It was painful to watch, but it illustrated the concept of the agony of defeat extremely well!

Sports offer many opportunities to experience the 'thrill of victory' and the 'agony of defeat'. Sometimes a star athlete can experience both of these polar emotions in the same season or even in the same game. Amazing victories can quickly fade into crushing defeats. Heroes can quickly become scapegoats. Everything can come crashing down quite rapidly.

The same thing can be said for life in general. Life is often like a rollercoaster with frequent highs and lows. If one lives long enough, he or she will likely experience the 'thrill of victory' and the 'agony of defeat' numerous times. Personal successes can quickly migrate into personal failures.

Life seems particularly hard when we are walking through the valley of the 'agony of defeat'. For some, this valley experience becomes persistent and long-lasting. In this valley we often experience a myriad of emotions like discouragement, dismay, disillusionment, depression and despair. But perhaps the most crippling emotion we encounter in the valley of the 'agony of defeat' is fear.

Fear is one of the most innate and powerful emotions in the human experience. Dictators and abusers know they can maintain power over others by creating fear in them. As the old adage goes: 'It is better to be feared than loved'. Fear can lead people to make poor decisions and to retreat into a stagnant existence.

> The power of fear is ... a threat to Christians, and can lead us to cease serving God faithfully.

The power of fear is also a threat to Christians, and can lead us to cease serving God faithfully. Therefore, Christians must learn to deal with fear.

Elijah was a man who understood fear and all of its crippling effects. Thus the things that happened to Elijah are useful in instructing us regarding how to deal with fear.

The thrill of victory: Elijah's great success

Elijah's most profound bout of fear occurred just on the heels of one of his greatest victories. During the early part of Elijah's ministry Israel was deeply immersed in idolatry. They had transferred their loyalty to the false gods Baal and Asherah. This idolatry was encouraged and supported by Jezebel who was then the Queen of Israel. To Elijah, and to God, this idolatry was an abomination and it had to come to an end.

In 1 Kings 18 Elijah challenged the prophets of Baal to a duel on Mount Carmel, and he summoned all of Israel to witness the event. When the people were assembled, Elijah walked before them and declared: 'How long will you waver between two opinions? If the LORD is God, follow him; but if Baal is God, follow him' (1 Kings 18:21). The people said nothing. They were unwilling to shift their allegiances from Baal to the living and true God.

Elijah then threw down the gauntlet. Although he was outnumbered 450 to 1, he issued a challenge to the prophets of Baal. He demanded that two bulls be brought forth and cut into pieces. Elijah then commanded that the pieces be placed on wood, but he forbade anyone to set fire to the wood. Next he declared his challenge to the prophets of Baal and to the people: 'Then you call on the name of your god, and I will call on the name of the LORD. The god who answers by fire — he is God' (1 Kings 18:24). Elijah's challenge was accepted.

Elijah allowed the prophets of Baal to go first. They called upon Baal repeatedly from morning until noon. They shouted at the top of their lungs. They danced feverishly around their altar. There was no response. Nothing happened. Elijah began to taunt them, '"Shout louder!" he said. "Surely he is a god! Perhaps he is deep in thought, or busy, or travelling. Maybe he is sleeping and must be awakened"' (1 Kings 18:27).

The prophets of Baal shouted even louder. They slashed themselves with their weapons and allowed their blood to flow from the wounds. They frantically prophesied into the evening, but there was no response and no answer. The people of Israel gradually began to lose interest in the prophets of Baal.

Elijah then called the people to gather around him. In their presence he repaired the altar of the one true God. Before he called upon the name of the Lord to send fire, he commanded the people to fill four large jars with water and to pour the water on the offering and on the wood. The people did as he said. He told them to do it again and they did. Finally, Elijah demanded they pour water on the wood and offering a third time, and they did.

Elijah had raised the stakes significantly by dousing the offering and the wood three times with water. But he wanted to demonstrate the unparallelled power of the living God. He then called upon the name of the Lord and the Lord sent fire which burned up the sacrifice, the wood, the stones, the soil and all the excess water gathered in a trench around the sacrifice (1 Kings 18:38). When the people saw this display of power they fell to the ground and cried out: 'The LORD — he is God! The LORD — he is God!' (1 Kings 18:39). The people rejected their idolatry and turned their hearts back to the Lord!

What a moment! What a victory! Elijah must have been beaming with joy and brimming with confidence. Against all seeming human odds, Elijah and his God had triumphed over the prophets of Baal and had turned the people of Israel from their idolatry. Elijah must have been feeling the thrill of victory! But Elijah's thrill of victory would not last very long. It would soon be exchanged for the agony of defeat.

The agony of defeat: Elijah's great failure

After his victory on Mount Carmel, Elijah and King Ahab went to see Jezebel. Ahab informed her about everything that Elijah had done (1 Kings 19:1). We cannot be sure what Elijah was thinking, but it is probable that he thought that Jezebel would have the same reaction as the rest of Israel. Perhaps he was expecting her to repent of her idolatry and return to the one true God. If that's what Elijah was expecting, he was soon to be sorely disappointed.

Jezebel did not respond with repentance, but rather with vengeance. She was infuriated by what Elijah had done and she sent a messenger to him to declare the following threat: 'May the gods deal with me, be it ever so severely, if by this time tomorrow I do not make your life like that of one of them' (19:2). When Elijah heard this news the Bible tells us that he was 'afraid' and that he 'ran for his life' (19:3).

Elijah had seen God work many miracles. He had even seen God raise a man from the dead through his ministry. He had just seen God's great power on Mount Carmel. But Elijah's confidence and assurance in God was destroyed by the threats of one woman. He had withstood the opposition of 450 prophets of Baal and the entire nation of Israel, but in the face of Jezebel's hostility Elijah ran for his life in fear.

Elijah ran into the desert to escape from Jezebel. There he became very distraught. He became so filled with dismay that he wanted to end his life. He cried out to God: '"I have had enough, LORD," he said. "Take my life; I am no better than my ancestors"' (1 Kings 19:4). Elijah had made the journey from the thrill of victory to the agony of defeat.

Lessons from the life of Elijah

Elijah's surrender to fear led him to make some poor choices which only served to exacerbate his fear. The poor choices he made out of fear also led him to experience other debilitating emotions like depression and despair. But Elijah's struggle with fear and the other emotions it produced can serve to instruct us how to deal with fear in our own lives. We can learn three lessons on dealing with fear from the things that happened to Elijah.

Lesson 1: Get rest, eat and don't isolate yourself!

The first lesson we learn about dealing with fear from the life of Elijah is the importance of attending to some very basic issues in our lives, particularly during times of great stress. Elijah's fear led him to make three foolish choices which only led to an increase in his fear and made his situation much worse.

First, Elijah's fear led him to neglect his need for physical rest. He had just come from a tiring ordeal with the prophets of Baal and then he ran a day's journey to the desert (1 Kings 19:4). He was physically exhausted and he eventually collapsed and fell asleep under a tree (19:5). Elijah's fear led him to deprive himself of rest and he pushed his body to the limits. In the midst of this exhaustion, he cried out to God to take his life. Physical exhaustion and sleep deprivation only serve to increase our fear and they contribute to other destructive emotions like anxiety and depression. Elijah's error reminds us that one way to deal with our fear is simply to get adequate physical rest for our bodies.

Elijah's fear also led him to neglect his body in a second way. His fear not only left him physically exhausted, but it also left him famished. Elijah's fearful dash into the desert resulted in him neglecting to provide proper nutrition to his body. God recognized Elijah's need for food and drink, and he sent an angel to him who provided Elijah with bread and a jar of water (19:6). Elijah ate and drank, and then he slept again. Elijah's error reminds us that one of the ways to deal with fear is to make sure we are getting adequate nutrition for our bodies.

Finally, Elijah also exacerbated his fear by isolating himself. When Elijah heard Jezebel's threat he bolted off alone into the desert. Instead of running to a friend or seeking counsel from God, Elijah ran away all alone. He chose to isolate himself. Fear is often worsened when we isolate ourselves from other people. God recognized Elijah's need for a friend and companion. At the end of his desert journey, God provided Elijah with a co-labourer in Elisha (19:16-18). Once again, Elijah's error teaches us that we can deal with our fear by making sure we are not isolating ourselves from others during times of calamity.

One of the best ways for us to restrain the power of fear, and all the negative emotions it spawns, is by following these three simple rules — get rest, eat right and associate with other people. My pastoral and other professional experience has demonstrated to me that these simple rules are frequently ignored. In pastoral counselling, I would focus on these basic issues as the first step in dealing with fear and anxiety. It is amazing how our fears can be quelled by simply getting proper sleep, following good nutrition and fellowshipping with others.

Lesson 2: Don't focus on your problems — focus on God!

A second lesson we learn from the things that happened to Elijah is that our fear is worsened when we focus on our problems. Elijah's fear was fuelled by focusing on Jezebel's threats rather than on God's power to deliver him from these threats. A. W. Pink wrote of Elijah,

> His eyes were fixed on the wicked and furious queen: his mind was occupied with her power and fury, and therefore his heart was filled with terror. Faith in God is the only deliverer from carnal fear.[1]

When Elijah became fixated on Jezebel's threats he began to make poor decisions, like running into the desert all alone. Focusing solely on his problems led Elijah to exhaust and isolate himself. How quickly Elijah had forgotten the powerful God who brought fire from heaven and triumphed over the prophets of Baal!

I must confess that I often behave much like Elijah. Like Elijah, I can quickly swing from the thrill of victory to the agony of defeat. I have too often bolted into the desert in the face of troubling news and threats. Finally, I also tend to replicate Elijah's pattern of focusing on my problems rather than on God's delivering power. When things go wrong in my life I quickly become obsessed with the problem. Sometimes my obsession is related to trying to solve the problem. Other times my obsession is related to worrying about it. Like Elijah, I become absorbed in the problem and I need to be shaken out of my fixation by the Holy Spirit, God's Word, my spouse, or a Christian friend. How about you? Are you like Elijah in times of trial? Are you quickly arrested in the chains of fear and does this lead you to obsess about your problems?

God is not pleased when our fearfulness leads us to fixate on our problems, particularly when this fixation leads us to neglect seeking and trusting in him. God does not like it when we allow our problems to take precedence over our spiritual dispositions. God wants us to trust in him in times of trial and to remember that he is sovereign over our circumstances, even our most difficult problems. God reminded Elijah of his sovereignty over all things when Elijah arrived at Mount Horeb.

Elijah hears a gentle whisper

When Elijah was in the desert, God directed him to Mount Horeb. This journey took Elijah forty days and forty nights to complete, during which time God provided for all his needs. Just like the nation of Israel, Elijah had his own wilderness wanderings. When Elijah arrived at Mount Horeb, God commanded him: 'Go out and stand on the mountain in the presence of the LORD, for the LORD is about to pass by' (1 Kings 19:11). Elijah did as he was commanded.

As Elijah stood on the mountaintop a great and powerful wind arose which tore mountains apart and shattered the rocks around him. But the Lord was not found in the wind. After the wind ceased, a great earthquake occurred; but the Lord was not found in the earthquake. Following the earthquake a great fire broke out; but the Lord was not in the fire. Finally, after the wind, earthquake and fire, Elijah heard a gentle whisper. God *was* found in the gentle whisper and he spoke to Elijah.

> God wants us to trust in him in times of trial ... he is sovereign over our circumstances, even our most difficult problems.

Why did God display all these mighty natural events and then reveal himself in a gentle whisper? God's purpose was to demonstrate to Elijah that God is sovereign over all things, but often chooses to reveal himself in unexpected ways. He was reminding Elijah that he controls events and that even Jezebel's actions are subject to the bounds of his sovereignty. He was also telling Elijah to avoid focusing on the calamities around him and instead to seek the Lord where he may be found. God was telling Elijah not to be fearful because God was in charge of his circumstances.

Don't grant too much power to your problems

We all struggle with problems in our lives. Sometimes we become obsessed with these problems. They are all we can see. This can lead us to believe that our problems are sovereign. Focusing our minds in this way will only enhance our fear, anxiety, despair and depression. It is normal and appropriate for us to have concerns over legitimate struggles, but when we engage in excessive worrying we grant too much power to our problems. Such excessive worrying only serves to harm us. Worrying cannot change our circumstances as Jesus reminds us in Matthew 6:27: 'Who of you by worrying can add a single hour to his life?' Only God can change our circumstances. So why waste our time with obsessing about our problems? We should place our focus on God because he controls all things and can deliver us from our circumstances.

When you feel overcome by fear and sense yourself slipping into a state of obsession over your problems, follow the admonition of the apostle Paul: 'Do not be anxious about anything, but in everything, by prayer and petition, with thanksgiving, present your requests to God' (Philippians 4:6). One way to deal with fear is to focus on God rather than on our problems.

Lesson 3: Don't focus on yourself — focus on others!

Elijah not only made the mistake of focusing on his problems, but he also made the mistake of focusing on himself. During difficult and fearful periods in our lives we are inclined to become more self-centred. Our circumstances seem to justify a greater level of selfishness and self-absorption. But when we narrow the focus to ourselves we risk worsening our fear. When we focus on ourselves the walls of our trials seem to close in on us at a much more rapid pace. This is exactly what happened to Elijah.

After Elijah arrived at Mount Horeb he went into a cave and fell asleep. The next morning God spoke to him: 'What are you doing here, Elijah?' (1 Kings 19:9). Elijah responded: 'I have been very zealous for the LORD God Almighty. The Israelites have rejected your covenant, broken down your altars, and put your prophets to death with the sword. I am the only one left, and now they are trying to kill me too' (19:10). Do you see Elijah's self-centredness in his response to God? He has convinced himself that it is all about him. He believes he is the *only* faithful servant of God remaining: 'I am the only one left' (19:10).

Elijah echoed this self-centredness after God revealed himself to him in a gentle whisper. At that time God asked Elijah the very same question he had asked him earlier in the cave: 'What are you doing here, Elijah?' (19:13). Elijah repeated his earlier answer: 'I have been very zealous for the LORD God Almighty. The Israelites have rejected your covenant, broken down your altars, and put your prophets to death with the sword. I am the only one left, and now they are trying to kill me too.' Once again Elijah claimed to be the 'only one left' (19:14).

But this time God did not allow Elijah to keep ruminating in a pool of his own self-pity. God responded to Elijah with a series of commands and a declaration that disproved Elijah's self-centred misconceptions:

> The LORD said to him, 'Go back the way you came, and go to the Desert of Damascus. When you get there, anoint Hazael king over Aram. Also, anoint Jehu son of Nimshi king over Israel, and anoint Elisha son of Shaphat from Abel Meholah to succeed you as prophet. Jehu will put to death any who escape the sword of Hazael, and Elisha will put to death any who escape the sword of Jehu. *Yet I reserve seven thousand in Israel* — all whose knees have not bowed down to Baal and all whose mouths have not kissed him'
>
> (1 Kings 19:15-18, emphasis mine).

In his response God demonstrated to Elijah that it is not all about him. God had other servants like Hazael, Jehu and Elisha. God had seven thousand other faithful servants who had not bowed their knees to Baal. God was saying to Elijah, 'It's not all about you.'

Elijah allowed himself to believe that he was alone in his suffering and service to God. He indulged in self-pity that led to a martyr complex. His self-centredness only resulted in making him more fearful and distraught. In the midst of our own trials we often do a similar thing. We fool ourselves into believing that we alone are suffering and that no one else can identify with our personal struggle. We allow ourselves to believe it is all about us. We lose sight of the bigger picture of what God is doing. This type of behaviour only serves to set us on a more rapid downward spiral of fear and despair. Instead of focusing on ourselves in such circumstances we need to turn our attention to others. We need to remind ourselves that there are others out there who are serving and suffering.

One of the ways we can deal with fear is by turning the focus away from ourselves and shifting it to other people. When we do this we end the spiral of self-absorption which so often causes and exacerbates our fears. When we do this we also fulfil the good and perfect will of God: 'Do nothing out of selfish ambition or vain conceit, but in humility consider others better than yourselves. Each of you should look not only to your own interests, but also to the interests of others. Your attitude should be the same as that of Christ Jesus' (Philippians 2:3-5).

A man like us

Elijah experienced the thrill of victory and the agony of defeat. He understood what it was like to struggle with debilitating fear. Elijah was not a superhero; he was human just like us. James reminds us of this truth in his epistle where he declares that Elijah was a 'man just like us' (James 5:17). It should encourage us to know that God can use imperfect vessels like Elijah, and you and me, in great ways. God didn't discard Elijah because he struggled with fear, but rather God ministered to him during this time and shook him out of his self-absorption.

But Elijah was not just a man like us in the sense that he also serves as a type of the Lord Jesus Christ. Like Elijah, Jesus spent forty days and forty nights in the wilderness. Like Elijah, Jesus knew what it was to be alone and under attack by the wicked threats of Satan. Like Elijah, Jesus understood what it was like to have people seek after his life. Finally, like Elijah, Jesus is a man just like us. He too understands the trials of our temptations and the full range of human emotions. But unlike Elijah and us, Jesus always kept his focus on the will of the Father and the needs of others. Jesus never bolted in the face of threats. Therefore, we know that he will never leave us in the midst of our despair. Jesus promised to be with us always, even to the end of the age (Matthew 28:18-20). God does not want us to live in fear, but to trust in him as our loving heavenly father: 'For you did not receive a spirit that makes you a slave again to fear, but you received the Spirit of sonship. And by him we cry, "Abba, Father"' (Romans 8:15).

Elijah was indeed a man like us. Like us, he needed the Saviour Jesus Christ to deliver him and redeem him. Elijah needed to fix his eyes on Jesus in order to make it through the trials of this world. The same holds true for us. The best way to deal with fear and despair is to look to Christ for joy and deliverance.

7.

What happened to Daniel:

dealing with a hostile world

Then the king ordered Ashpenaz, chief of his court officials, to bring in some of the Israelites from the royal family and the nobility — young men without any physical defect, handsome, showing aptitude for every kind of learning, well informed, quick to understand, and qualified to serve in the king's palace. He was to teach them the language and literature of the Babylonians (Daniel 1:3-4).

One of the most challenging issues faced by Christian parents is how much they should allow their children to interact with the hostile and unbelieving world around them. Should they allow their children to watch that programme on television? Should they allow their children to use social networking sites on the Internet? Should they allow their children to have unbelieving friends? Every Christian parent wrestles with questions like these.

Of course, the struggle with how much to interact with the world is not limited to our children. Unless you are living in a monastery, every Christian encounters this challenge at some level every single day. Thankfully, most Christians do not face physical hostility from the world because of their faith, but we all face intellectual, or world view, hostility. The unbelieving world around us is like an orchestra which is following an entirely different conductor from the Christian. Whereas the Christian's world view is guided by the Word of God, the world view of the world is guided by personal preference, self-interest and the influence of the evil one.

Every time we venture from our homes, go to work, surf the Internet or turn on the television we mingle with the values and ideas of a hostile world. Since there is no way to avoid interacting with the world, the question we face as Christians is: how can we remain faithful while interacting with the world? I think we find some answers to these questions in the life of Daniel. The things that happened to Daniel can help instruct us regarding how we should deal with the hostile world around us.

Daniel *contra mundum*

The fourth-century church father Athanasius was constantly in battle against his enemies, most of whom were promoters of heresy. Athanasius faced relentless hostility from the world. He was persecuted by his opponents and was even twice exiled by them. He was so famous for his struggles against his adversaries that the following title was bestowed upon him: 'Athanasius *contra mundum*' ('Athanasius against the world'). Like Athanasius, Daniel's life was also lived *contra mundum*. He too was continually in conflict with the world around him.

Unlike Athanasius, however, Daniel had no choice but to interact with a hostile world. The biblical account of his life begins with this statement: 'In the third year of the reign of Jehoiakim king of Judah, Nebuchadnezzar king of Babylon came to Jerusalem and besieged it' (Daniel 1:1). Daniel was taken prisoner by the Babylonians. He was forced to live in a world that was entirely contrary to all he held so dear. He was compelled to live in a world that was hostile to his faith. In Babylon, Daniel received a hostile education and was immersed in a hostile culture.

A hostile education

The Babylonians were a sophisticated people and they understood how to operate an empire. They knew that their education system could be used as a tool for maintaining their empire. They understood that education can shape a child's world view for the rest of his or her life. Therefore, when the Babylonians besieged Jerusalem they took Israel's most gifted children captive so that they could be educated in the school of Babylon:

> Then the king ordered Ashpenaz, chief of his court officials, to bring in some of the Israelites from the royal family and the nobility — young men without any physical defect, handsome, showing aptitude for every kind of learning, well informed, quick to understand, and qualified to serve in the king's palace. He was to teach them the language and literature of the Babylonians
>
> (Daniel 1:3-4).

Babylon took Israel's brightest and best, and among them was Daniel.

In the school of Babylon Daniel encountered a hostile world. Instead of learning the Hebrew language and the Hebrew Scriptures, Daniel was forced to learn 'the language and literature of the Babylonians' (1:4). It is likely that Daniel was schooled in the occult, magic, astrology and polytheism. He received this training for a period of three years (1:5).

The entire purpose of the Babylonian educational system was to assimilate Daniel and these other young Israelites into thinking like Babylonians so that they would be useful to the needs of the empire. Daniel was being trained to serve the King of Babylon instead of God. The Babylonians even changed Daniel's name to reflect their goal. The name 'Daniel' means 'my judge is God'. The Babylonians changed Daniel's name to 'Belteshazzar' which means 'protect the king'. The education Daniel received in Babylon was aimed at placing a new king over Daniel's life. Daniel received an education that was entirely hostile to his faith.

A hostile culture

But the hostility Daniel encountered in Babylon was not limited to his education. Daniel also encountered a hostile culture when he was outside the classroom. The Babylonians were not content with transforming how Daniel thought; they also wanted to transform how he lived his life. The Babylonians endeavoured to assimilate Daniel into their culture.

One way the Babylonians tried to do this was by giving him a seat at the king's table and allowing him to eat the king's food (Daniel 1:5). While eating the king's food represented a violation of Israel's dietary laws, the true hostility encountered here by Daniel runs much deeper than that. The Babylonians wanted Daniel to eat the rich food of the king so that he would become indebted to this pagan king for his health and well-being. Daniel obstinately refused to become indebted to the king in this manner and so he ate only vegetables. Daniel wanted to make sure that his allegiance was to God and not to the King of Babylon (Daniel 1:11-16). But the purpose of the Babylonians was clear. They attempted to use the king's table as a way of enticing Daniel into their culture.

A second way the Babylonians tried to assimilate Daniel into their culture was by attempting to force him to adopt

Babylonian religious practices. The Babylonians accomplished this through the forceful hand of the state. The King of Babylon issued a decree demanding that everyone worship an image of gold. When the music played in Babylon, all the citizens were required to prostrate themselves before this idolatrous national image. Disobedience to this decree carried the penalty of death in a fiery furnace. The Babylonians took this religious inculcation a step further when they enacted a law that prohibited praying to anyone except the king. These laws were blatantly hostile to the practice of Daniel's faith.

The Babylonians attempted to entice and force Daniel into conforming to their culture through the invitation to dine at the king's table and through the decree regarding worshipping the image of gold. In Babylon, Daniel encountered a culture which was hostile to his faith.

Lessons from the life of Daniel

As we have seen, Daniel was forced to interact with a world that was hostile to his faith. He was immersed into the Babylonian world, a world in direct opposition to his own. In fact, Babylon was so antithetical to the true Israelite religion that the name 'Babylon' eventually emerged as a biblical metaphor for systems and governments that stand in opposition to the kingdom of God (1 Peter 5:13; Revelation 14:8; 16:19; 17:5; 18:2, 10 & 21). The Babylonians attempted to train Daniel to think, act and worship like them. Yet, Daniel maintained his faith even in the midst of this focused and concerted effort to undermine it.

The question for us is: what can we learn from Daniel's experiences in Babylon and how can we apply them in the age in which we live? The things that happened to Daniel can teach us many things about interacting with the hostile world that surrounds us. Here are three lessons from Daniel's life regarding dealing with the hostile world.

Lesson 1: The world seeks to change us

Daniel's life teaches us that one of the world's goals is to change us. Daniel's experience in Babylon is a typical example of how the world as an anti-God system seeks to conform our minds to its ways. The way the world seeks to do this is by changing how we think and what we worship.

The first thing the Babylonians tried to do was to educate Daniel according to their knowledge. They wanted Daniel to think like a Babylonian. The methods of the world have not changed. Our world seeks to indoctrinate us into thinking and reasoning according to its standards rather than according to God's standards. In the public classrooms and on the airwaves, our modern world is attempting to convince us to think like the world.

The Babylonians also tried to change Daniel's allegiance to God by enticing him to sit at the king's table and by prohibiting him from worshipping God. The world employs the same twin-attack strategies on the Christian today. As with Daniel, the world attempts to seduce us with its wealth and power. The world is constantly inviting us to eat from its table of luxuries. The apostle John accurately summarizes what the world has to offer: 'For everything in the world — the cravings of sinful man, the lust of his eyes and the boasting of what he has and does — comes not from the Father *but from the world*' (1 John 2:16, emphasis mine). The world has an insatiable appetite for our conformity and it works tirelessly to seduce us in that direction. It longs for us to attribute our well-being to the things it has to offer. It desires our allegiance.

> The world has an insatiable appetite for our conformity and it works tirelessly to seduce us in that direction.

I've experienced the world's seductive powers many times in my life. One of the times I faced such seductive powers was just after I graduated from law school. After graduation I joined a very large law firm. In the prestigious halls of a large law firm the lure of worldly power and money is everywhere. Fancy cars and fine clothes were the rewards for hard labour. It was easy for me to be convinced that I was deserving of such luxuries and I was certainly encouraged to partake of them. The lure of the king's table is a difficult thing to resist. Our modern-day Babylon is constantly calling us to worship its golden statue, an idol composed of an amalgamation of sex, money and power.

But the world not only seeks to change our allegiance by calling us to worship these false gods, it also does so by restricting our ability to worship the one true God. Just as Babylon attempted to prohibit the public exercise of Daniel's faith by limiting his ability to pray to God, our world is constantly trying to get us to restrict our religious expression in the public square. The world tells us that our faith is solely a private matter. It demands that our faith have no voice in the halls of government and the classrooms of our schools.

The world has an overarching and indefatigable goal of changing how we think and what we worship. The things that happened to Daniel serve as a stark warning to us to be on guard because the world seeks to change us.

Lesson 2: We can change the world

While Daniel's life is filled with warnings about how the world seeks to change us, his life also teaches us that we can sometimes change the world. By interacting with the hostile world around him, Daniel was able to influence the hearts of two unbelieving kings — Darius and Nebuchadnezzar.

Daniel became one of King Darius' administrators. In fact, Scripture testifies that Daniel was his most useful, effective and favourite administrator (Daniel 6:3). Daniel excelled in his occupation as an administrator in the government of a pagan king! His success gained him the respect of Darius, which was to prove quite valuable to Daniel when he was thrown into a den of lions. When Darius learned that Daniel's life was at risk, Scripture records his response: 'When the king heard this, he was greatly distressed; he was determined to rescue Daniel and made every effort until sundown to save him' (6:14). Through his interaction with the hostile world around him Daniel was able to change the heart and behaviour of Darius. Daniel was used by God to soften the heart of Darius, making him more favourable to the needs of God's people.

Even more impressive was how Daniel impacted the life of King Nebuchadnezzar. As with Darius, Daniel gained access and influence with Nebuchadnezzar because of his effectiveness and knowledge. Nebuchadnezzar was a very proud man and he believed his great empire was achieved entirely by his own efforts. King Nebuchadnezzar failed to acknowledge the greatness and sovereignty of the true God, but Daniel, through his interaction with the king, served as a constant witness to the true God. Eventually, God used this witness and intervened in the life of Nebuchadnezzar. This pagan king came to his senses and began to praise God rather than himself. Nebuchadnezzar actually became a herald of the mighty acts of God. Daniel 4 records his proclamation:

It is my pleasure to tell you about the miraculous signs and wonders that the Most High God has performed for me.

How great are his signs,
how mighty his wonders!
His kingdom is an eternal kingdom;
his dominion endures from
generation to generation

(Daniel 4:2-3).

By interacting with the hostile world around him Daniel was used by God to bring light to the mind of King Nebuchadnezzar.

This dynamic of believers changing the world around them can also be seen in the courageous faithfulness of Daniel's three companions, Shadrach, Meshach and Abednego. Like Daniel, these three men were torn from their cultural moorings and forced into the indoctrination of the Babylonian system. But, like Daniel, they never ceased to live faithfully in the midst of a hostile world and like Daniel they changed the world. For example, when King Nebuchadnezzar attempted to force Shadrach, Meshach and Abednego to worship his golden image the three young men refused to comply declaring they would never serve false gods (Daniel 3:16-18). Their defiance earned them the punishment of being cast into a fiery furnace. But because of their faithfulness, God delivered them from this peril. The courageous stand taken by these three men, and the powerful deliverance they experienced by God, was used by God to change the heart orientation of King Nebuchadnezzar:

> Then Nebuchadnezzar said, 'Praise be to the God of Shadrach, Meshach and Abednego, who has sent his angel and rescued his servants! They trusted in him and defied the king's command and were willing to give up their lives rather than serve or worship any god except their own God. Therefore I decree that the people of any nation or language who say anything against the God of Shadrach, Meshach and Abednego be cut into pieces and their houses be turned into piles of rubble, for no other god can save in this way'
>
> (Daniel 3:28-29).

By living faithfully in the midst of a hostile world, Shadrach, Meshach and Abednego were able to change the world.

Daniel and his companions were able to change the world by interacting with it. Their worldly education and worldly positions allowed them to serve God in great ways. As Christians we experience similar opportunities every day as we interact with the world. In fact, Jesus specifically commissions us with the task of changing the world around us.

In the Sermon on the Mount, Jesus commanded us to be salt and light in the world (Matthew 5:13-14). He demanded that we not put our light under a basket, but rather he called the church to be a shining city on a hill (5:14-16). Jesus commissioned his church to proclaim his good news and 'go and make disciples of all nations' (28:18-20). There is a gospel imperative to interact with the hostile world around us. Isn't this exactly what the apostles did? Isn't this the story of the book of Acts? In Acts we find Paul, much like Daniel and his companions, trying to influence and change the hearts of pagan rulers. As Christians, we are all called to change the world through proclaiming and living the power of the gospel. The things that happened to Daniel remind us that by interacting with the world we can sometimes change the world.

Lesson 3: We have overcome the world

Finally, Daniel's life also teaches us that by interacting with a hostile world we can learn the lesson that, through Christ, we have overcome the world. The world is a powerful and multi-faceted enemy. We should be appropriately fearful of its power to undermine our faith. After all, the apostle Paul reminds us that we need the full complement of spiritual armour when interacting with the world: 'For our struggle is not against flesh and blood, but against the rulers, against the authorities, against the powers of *this dark world* and against the spiritual forces of evil in the heavenly realms' (Ephesians 6:12, emphasis mine).

Every Christian must face the powers of this dark world and that is a fearful reality.

Daniel faced the powers of this dark world in vivid and memorable ways. These powers threw him into a lion's den, and cast his companions into a fiery furnace. But the message of Daniel's life is that God overcomes the powers of this dark world. Daniel was delivered from the lion's den and his companions were delivered from the fiery furnace. The kings who attempted to use their worldly powers to change the heart and mind of Daniel and his companions were themselves changed by the power of God. The ultimate message of the book of Daniel is that God is sovereign over kings, nations, peoples and history. God can shut the mouths of lions and he can make men survive blistering flames. God overcame the world for Daniel and he does the same for all his children.

God's victory over the world was sealed and completed through the work of Jesus Christ. In his farewell discourse, Jesus encouraged his disciples with these words: 'I have told you these things, so that in me you may have peace. In this world you will have trouble. But take heart! *I have overcome the world*' (John 16:33, emphasis mine). The apostle John informs us that Jesus' glorious victory over the world extends to everyone who believes in Jesus: 'Who is it that overcomes the world? Only he who believes that Jesus is the Son of God' (1 John 5:5).

> Because of the victory of Jesus we engage the world with the protection of his armour.

The knowledge that Jesus has overcome the world, and that we have overcome the world through him, should provide us with great comfort as we deal with a hostile world each day. Because of the victory of Jesus we engage the world with the protection of his armour. We wear the belt of *his* truth, the breastplate of *his* righteousness, the footwear of *his* gospel of peace, the shield of *his* faith, the helmet of *his* salvation and the sword of *his* Spirit (Ephesians 6:14-17). We wear this armour in the workplace and in the universities. We wear it in the public square. We dress our children in this armour.

Yes, the battle is real. Yes, the enemy is powerful. But as we live in this hostile world we are comforted by the knowledge that it has been overcome by King Jesus. The serpent may have bruised Jesus' heel, but Jesus has crushed its head. This world is Jesus' domain. Jesus has overcome the world and through our union with him we too have overcome the world. The things that happened to Daniel comfort us with the knowledge that we have overcome the world through Jesus Christ.

Seeing the Son of Man

One of the gifts God gave to Daniel was the ability to interpret dreams. One of the dreams Daniel interpreted included a prophecy regarding future empires and kings. God enabled Daniel to predict the coming of future empires such as Greece and Rome. But the most amazing part of Daniel's interpretation of this dream was that it contained a prophecy regarding the coming of Jesus Christ. Daniel foretold of a coming kingdom that would surpass all the preceding and subsequent kingdoms of this world (Daniel 7:23). He described the King of this coming kingdom as the 'Ancient of Days' and 'one like a son of man' (7:13). This coming King foretold by Daniel is the Lord Jesus Christ.

As Daniel's life teaches us, interacting with a hostile world is no easy task. At times, the powers of this dark world will win occasional battles, but because of the kingship of Jesus Christ the war has been won and our victory is assured. The things that happened to Daniel serve as a reminder to us that when we struggle with dealing with the hostile world in which we live we must look to the risen and victorious Christ. Like Daniel, in the midst of trial and tribulation we must see the Son of Man and cling to the knowledge that through him we have overcome the world.

8.

What happened to David:

dealing with death

David pleaded with God for the child. He fasted and went into his house and spent the nights lying on the ground. The elders of his household stood beside him to get him up from the ground, but he refused, and he would not eat any food with them. On the seventh day the child died. David's servants were afraid to tell him that the child was dead, for they thought, 'While the child was still living, we spoke to David but he would not listen to us. How can we tell him the child is dead? He may do something desperate'
(2 Samuel 12:16-18).

Almost every Christian is familiar with the following words spoken by the apostle Paul: 'For to me, to live is Christ and to die is gain' (Philippians 1:21). In theory, all Christians believe the truth of that statement, but in practice many of us have a hard time living it. For most of us, death is one of the most fearful and painful experiences of human existence. When we lose a loved one to death it is excruciatingly painful. On this side of glory, death appears to us as only a gigantic loss.

It leaves an indelible crater in our souls. Dealing with death is incredibly difficult.

The difficulty of dealing with death for the Christian is further complicated by what we believe. We believe that death is a 'home-going' for the believer. We believe that the soul of the believing loved one has gone to the bosom of Christ while his or her body awaits the resurrection. Because we believe these things, we struggle with whether it is appropriate to mourn the passing of one who has just gone to such a great reward. But, at the same time, we struggle with the sadness we have over the loss. Should we celebrate death as a 'home-going', or mourn death as a loss? Christians often struggle to find the appropriate response to death.

One of the ways we can discover how Christians should deal with death is by looking at the life of David. David faced many sorrows in his life, but perhaps the greatest one was the death of his unnamed infant son. In this chapter we'll explore David's loss and how he responded to it. We'll look at the things that happened to David and discern what he can teach us about dealing with death.

David loses a son

While David experienced the death of other children, like Absalom, the death of his unnamed infant son carried the greatest sting because of the circumstances that gave rise to his death. David's infant son died because of David's personal sin.

In an act of lust and greed, David convinced himself that he needed another man's wife. After seeing Bathsheba bathing on a rooftop, David summoned her to his palace. He not only committed adultery with Bathsheba, but he also proceeded to arrange for the death of Bathsheba's husband Uriah. David made certain that the loyal Uriah was placed in a dangerous position in battle, thus ensuring his death. David committed adultery and murder.

God was angered over David's sins and he sent the prophet Nathan to convict David of his wrongdoing. Through a parable, Nathan revealed to David what he had done. When David's eyes were open to his sin he immediately proclaimed: 'I have sinned against the LORD' (2 Samuel 12:13). God spared David's life, but he told David that his punishment would include the death of the son he had conceived with Bathsheba (12:14).

David faced devastating news. He was about to experience one of the most painful things imaginable — the death of a child. What he did in response to this extraordinarily painful death is instructive for our lives. David had three responses to the death of his son which can serve to guide us when we are dealing with death.

Lesson 1: We need to mourn … for a time

One of the lessons we learn from David's ordeal with death is the importance of mourning and grieving. It is appropriate and necessary for us to respond to death with grieving. Godly men 'mourned deeply' as they buried the martyr Stephen (Acts 8:2). Our Lord wept at the death of his friend Lazarus (John 11:35) even though he knew that he would soon raise him from the dead. In order to deal with death, we must make time for mourning our loss.

David was a man who had frequent occasions to mourn. When David learned that his best friend Jonathan had died in battle, David responded with mourning: 'Then David and all the men with him took hold of their clothes and tore them. They mourned and wept and fasted till evening for Saul and his son Jonathan,' (2 Samuel 1:11-12). David even wrote a song of lament to honour the passing of Saul and Jonathan (1:19-27). David also mourned over the death of his rebellious son Absalom.

When David learned of Absalom's death he was 'shaken' by the news and he 'wept' saying, 'O my son Absalom! My son, my son Absalom! If only I had died instead of you — O Absalom, my son, my son!' (18:33).

While David had many occasions to mourn in his life, his most fervent episode of mourning occurred at the death of his infant son. Perhaps this was because of the young age of the child and because David's own sins had led to his child's death.

Because God had revealed ahead of time that his son would die, David's mourning and grieving occurred while the child was still sick. He mourned before his death, knowing that it was coming. Although the timing of David's mourning was different from what we usually experience, it still serves as a great example of the human need to mourn the loss of a loved one.

David's time of mourning

David's mourning and grieving manifested itself in a variety of ways. He refused to eat anything (2 Samuel 12:16). He spent his nights lying on the ground and the elders were unable to get him up (12:16-17). He became so despondent during this period of grieving that his servants feared telling him of his son's death because they thought he might do something desperate (12:18). David's mourning was severe and intense, impacting him physically and emotionally.

> Every time someone dies we are faced with the ugly reminder of the consequences of human sin.

Like David, we need to grieve over the pain of death and this grieving process will also impact us physically and emotionally. It is proper for Christians to be saddened by death because it is an abnormality in God's created world. Prior to the fall of mankind death was unknown to humanity. We were not created to die. Human sin brought death into the world. As the apostle Paul reminds us in Romans 6:23: 'For the wages of sin is death.' Every time someone dies we are faced with the ugly reminder of the consequences of human sin. These realities should make us grieve and mourn.

But the reasons why we need to grieve are not just theological, they are also personal and existential. Humans were created by God to be relational and social beings. God made us this way because he is a relational and social being. God exists in a glorious Trinity wherein there is mutual love and communion among the three persons of the Godhead. His very nature reveals that he is relational. God also chose to enter into a covenant relationship with man. God bound himself in relationship with humanity.

Given that God is a relational being, it is not surprising that his image-bearers share this characteristic. God made us to live in relationship with other human beings. We experience these relationships on a variety of levels, but none more intimate than those of marriage and family. The most profound forms of human interconnectedness are experienced in our marriages and in our families. Thus when we lose a spouse, a parent, a sibling, or a child, something is torn from the fabric of our being. Similar feelings are experienced when we lose a lifelong friend. Such intimate losses are extremely painful and it is necessary for us to give voice to that grief through mourning. It is also appropriate for other Christians to join us in mourning our losses. The apostle Paul commands us to 'mourn with those who mourn' (Romans 12:15).

Mourning and grieving over death allows us to reflect upon the dire consequences of sin and to voice the pain of loss which is tearing at the fabric of our hearts. In the wake of death, Christians are not called to be stoic, maintaining a stiff upper lip, but rather we are called to be expressive in our sorrow over the ravages of the great enemy named death. This is exactly what David did when losing his son.

David's mourning comes to an end

But it is important to note that David's time of mourning was finite and relatively short. His mourning was but for a time. He agonized over the death of his son for seven days, but then his mourning ended and David began to live again.

When David's period of mourning ended he began resuming his life by picking himself up off the floor. He then washed, put on lotions and changed his clothes. He worshipped God and ate food at his own table (2 Samuel 12:20). Later he comforted his wife Bathsheba and was sexually intimate with her (12:24). The fruit of their time together was another son who would be named Solomon. Soon after his mourning ended, David also began attending to his kingly duties by amassing an army and waging war (12:29-30). After his period of mourning, David began living, worshipping, loving and serving again.

Here David teaches us an important lesson about mourning. He reminds us that our mourning must not be indefinite or pro-longed. While it is proper for us to be devastated by death and to be driven to the floor by it, there comes a time when we need to pick ourselves up and return to serving God and others. It may take longer for us than David's seven days, but there comes a point when we wash, change our clothes and live again.

Why must we live again? We must live again because God commands us to use our days in service to him and to others. He calls us to live again because it testifies to our belief that death has been conquered through the work of Jesus Christ. Yes, we need to mourn, but only for a time. Like with David, there comes a time when we must cease mourning the dead and resume living for Jesus.

Lesson 2: We need to stay close to God

A second lesson we glean from David's ordeal with death is that we need to stay close to God at times of great loss. When we are dealing with death we need to make sure that we draw near to God through prayer and worship.

God had levied a heavy punishment on David. As a consequence of David's sins, God took the life of his son. But David did not react to this tremendously difficult providence by cutting off communication with God. Instead, David stayed close to God both during his ordeal and in its aftermath.

During the period of his son's illness, David sought the face of God in prayer (2 Samuel 12:16). He prayed that God would spare the life of his son. Even though God had pronounced judgement, David did not give up seeking God in prayer. In 2 Samuel 12:22, David explains why he prayed even in the face of God's decree: 'Who knows? The LORD may be gracious to me and let the child live.' David understood that God is gracious. He grasped this reality even in the midst of a very difficult time. David stayed close to God in prayer and affirmed God's gracious nature.

After his son died, David continued to stay close to God. One of the things David did immediately after his son's death was to go to the house of the Lord and worship God (2 Samuel 12:20). He also quickly resumed serving God as his anointed king (12:29-30). David never allowed the pain of death, which he knew came directly from God's hand, to lead to alienation from God.

When we deal with death it is easy for us to allow ourselves to step away from God. We can become cold to him because we blame him for death. Many people reject God during times of loss. For many, death is the destroyer of faith. After Job lost all that he had, including the lives of his children, he was in a deep period of mourning. He may have been tempted to reject God entirely in the wake of his extreme loss. His wife even encouraged him to do so, declaring to him: 'Are you still holding on to your integrity? Curse God and die!' (Job 2:9). But Job did not curse God. He did become frustrated and did question God's decisions, but even in these responses he remained close to God. Even expressing our pain and anger to God is a way to stay near him. Throughout his ordeal, Job never strayed from the throne of God. Eventually, through his communication with God, Job found answers to his questions, and peace regarding his circumstances. Like David, Job stayed close to God even during an extremely painful providence.

I understand the temptation to move away from God at a time of loss. I lost my father to cancer. He was only fifty-six years old. I watched him deteriorate and saw the savageness of our enemy. I can recall the range of emotions I experienced during that time. My emotions journeyed from sadness, to despair and, finally, to anger. One time my anger spilled over into my prayer life as I, like Job, questioned God's wisdom and providence. But, by God's grace, I never drifted from my Father's throne. God met me often in that time. He ministered to me through the comfort of other Christians. He spoke to me through his Word preached. He displayed to me the hope of the gospel through the sacrament of the Lord's Supper. He fed me in the wilderness. He sustained me.

The things that happened to David remind us that we must not allow death to cause us to drift away from God. David trusted in a gracious God even when circumstances seemed to indicate otherwise. David stayed close to God.

Lesson 3: We need to remember that death causes only a temporary separation

The final, and most important, lesson we learn from David about dealing with death is that it causes only a temporary separation. Because of the victory of Jesus Christ over the grave, death can only exact temporary pain. When we lose a loved one who was a believer we know that they are immediately with Christ and that someday we will be reunited with them.

David understood this reality even before the death and resurrection of Jesus. He testified to it as he explained why he ceased mourning over the death of his son: 'But now that he is dead, why should I fast? Can I bring him back again? *I will go to him, but he will not return to me*' (2 Samuel 12:23, emphasis mine). David understood that his son would not come back to him, but that he would one day go to him. David understood that death is not the end.

The reality that death causes only a temporary separation between us and those we have lost should provide great comfort to those who remain behind. It should provide us comfort because we realize that our loss results in unspeakable gain to the one we have lost. Those that we have lost in this age are now in the blissful presence of Christ. This is why Paul said, 'For to me, to live is Christ *and to die is gain*' (Philippians 1:21, emphasis mine). Paul understood that death is an advantage to the one called home to Christ. The dead in Christ are healed of their illnesses and their tears have been wiped away. What comfort fills the heart of those who mourn in this age when they think of their beloved in the glorious presence of the living God!

> What comfort fills the heart of those who mourn in this age when they think of their beloved in the glorious presence of the living God!

But the reality that death results in only a temporary separation should also comfort us because we know that someday we will be reunited with those we have lost. The Puritan Matthew Henry writes:

The consideration of our own death should moderate our sorrow at the death of our relations. It is the common lot; instead of mourning for their death, we should think of our own: and, whatever loss we have of them now, we shall die shortly, and go to them.[1]

We are separated from those we love for only for a season. When we grasp this truth it helps us to cease our mourning and return to living.

David was able to make the transition out of his state of mourning because he understood that death results in only a temporary separation. He grasped the concept that while he would not see his son again in this life, he would indeed see him again. David also knew that his departed son was in the presence of a holy God. His son had gone to the place prepared for him by the Lord Jesus Christ (John 14:1-4). David could go on living because he knew that Paul's words applied to him and to his son: 'For to me, to live is Christ, and to die is gain' (Philippians 1:21).

The Son who lives

Death is the great equalizer. No one, regardless of their wealth and power, can escape it. Nearly everyone reading this chapter has been, or will be, confronted with the painful loss of a loved one.

The things that happened to David help us to respond to death in a biblical manner. First, we rightfully mourn the loss of those we love. But we also recognize that this mourning should come to an end because we believe death is not the end for those who are in Christ Jesus. Second, throughout the dying process and in its aftermath we remain close to God. We need to pray to him, worship him and, at times, appropriately share our hurts and anger with him. Finally, we must remember that death creates only a temporary separation between us and the departed in Christ. One day we will go to them and we know that while we wait for this great reunion they remain in the bosom of Christ.

While all of these lessons are helpful for dealing with death, none will entirely remove its pain for us. We will miss those we have lost. But what should carry us through this pain is the reality of the resurrection of Jesus Christ. David was not the only father who lost a son: 'For God so loved the world that he gave his one and only Son, that whoever believes in him shall not perish but have eternal life' (John 3:16). The way we deal with death is by reminding ourselves of the biblical truth that Jesus has conquered death. We ultimately deal with death by looking to the Son who lives and because he lives we will live also (John 14:19). When we focus upon the victory of Jesus over the grave, we can come to grasp the meaning of Paul's words in a new and powerful way. We can join Paul in affirming: 'For to me, to live is Christ and to die is gain.'

Notes

Introduction

1. Dutch theologian J. Douma as quoted in Sidney Greidanus, *Sola Scriptura* (Toronto, Canada: Wedge Publishing, 1970), 43.

Chapter 1

1. Wilhelmus a Brakel, *The Christian's Reasonable Service*, trans. Bartel Elshout, vol. 3 (Pittsburgh, PA: Soli Deo Gloria Publications, 1994), 420.

2. Iain Duguid, *Living in the Gap Between Promise and Reality: The Gospel According to Abraham* (Philippsburg, NJ: P & R Publishing, 1999), 64-65.

3. Wilhelmus a Brakel, *The Christian's Reasonable Service*, trans. Bartel Elshout, vol. 2 (Pittsburgh, PA: Soli Deo Gloria Publications, 1994), 630-631.

Chapter 3

1. Melinda Beck, 'If at First You Don't Succeed, You're in Excellent Company,' *The Wall Street Journal*, 29 April 2008, page D1.

Chapter 6

1. A.W. Pink, *Elijah* (Carlisle, PA: Banner of Truth, 2002), 196.

Chapter 8

1. Matthew Henry's commentary on 2 Samuel 12:23 from www.ccel.org.

Other books by the author...

What
the Bible
teaches about
marriage

There is no question that our world today suffers from high divorce rates, rampant sexual promiscuity and a free and easy attitude to relationships. While we can blame the presence of sin as a reason for this, it does not wholly explain why many Christians seem to struggle with the same sexual and marital problems as the world.

In the belief that this is partly due to the failure of the church to instruct its people about the true nature of redeemed relationships, Anthony Selvaggio takes a thoroughly biblical and immensely practical look at the topics of human sexuality, romance and marriage, as they are revealed in the Song of Songs. It is his desire that marriages will be restored and enriched as we examine this picture of the divine love of God expressed in the greatest love of all, the Lord Jesus Christ.

What the Bible teaches about marriage, EP Books, 240 pages, ISBN-13: 978-0-85234-634-12.

The 24/7 Christian

Do you ever struggle? Are you sometimes tempted to throw in the towel? Do you long for Christ to return? You are not alone, and thankfully you have been left with help and certain hope as you press on in your Christian walk.

The book of James is immensely controversial to some (ask Martin Luther), yet Anthony Selvaggio expertly opens up and shows us that this part of God's inspired Word is as relevant to each of us right now as it was to the struggling Christians late in the first century.

You will find that James' letter is one of pastoral concern to the scattered Christians who suffered a great deal of persecution, and who faced many challenges every day just as we do. His intention is to be practical and encouraging, yet there is also stern warning and a plea for them to get their focus right and to live like Christians, putting their faith to work as they wait patiently for Christ's second coming.

Professing Jesus is simply not enough; we must live like Jesus as well. And not just on Sundays, but 24/7.

The 24/7 Christian, EP Books, 176 pages, ISBN-13: 978-0-85234-687-7.

The prophets speak of him

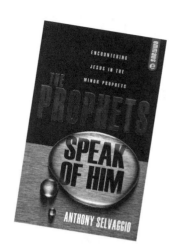

The Minor Prophets are an important but often neglected part of the Bible. The corpus which constitutes the Minor Prophets includes twelve books written by twelve different prophets. Due to the number of books, they were historically referred to as 'The Book of the Twelve' or simply 'The Twelve'. Today, they are most commonly referred to as the 'Minor Prophets'. It is important to note, however, that they are not referred to as 'minor' because they lack theological significance, but this title rather reflects the relatively short length of their individual prophecies. In fact, these twelve books are anything but minor. They are filled with tremendously deep and rich theological material. The Minor Prophets will certainly not prove minor to any reader who will invest the time to explore them.

While the Minor Prophets speak to a vast array of issues, this book is particularly focused on what they have to say about Jesus Christ. Why is the focus on Jesus Christ? It is because Jesus is the central figure of the entire Bible. The entire Bible speaks of him, including the Minor Prophets. Simply stated, the Bible is ultimately about Jesus Christ and his redemptive work.

The prophets speak of him, EP Books, ISBN-13: 978-0-85234-612-9, 208 pages.